IS YOU OKAY?

IS YOU OKAY?

GLOZELL GREEN

with NILS PARKER

HarperOne
An Imprint of HarperCollins*Publishers*

HarperOne

HarperCollins books may be purchased for educational, business, or sales promotional use. For information, please email the Special Markets Department at SPsales@harpercollins.com.

FIRST EDITION

Designed by Terry McGrath

Library of Congress Cataloging-in-Publication Data

Names: Green, GloZell.
Title: Is you okay? / GloZell Green ; with Nils Parker.
Description: First edition. I New York, NY : HarperOne, 2016.
Identifiers: LCCN 2016011727 (print) I LCCN 2016013707 (ebook) I ISBN 9780062459428 (hardback) I ISBN 9780062560346 (audio) I ISBN 9780062459411 (ebook)
Subjects: LCSH: Green, GloZell, 1972- I YouTube (Electronic resource)—Biography. I Video blogs—United States—Biography. I Internet users—United States—Biography. I Women comedians—United States—Biography. I Life skills. I BISAC: SELF-HELP / Motivational & Inspirational. I SELF-HELP / Personal Growth / Happiness. I SELF-HELP / Personal Growth / Success.
Classification: LCC TK5105.8868.Y68 G57 2016 (print) I LCC TK5105.8868.Y68 (ebook) I DDC 792.702/8092 [B]—dc23 LC record available at https://lccn.loc .gov/2016011727

ISBN 978-0-06-245942-8

16 17 18 19 20 RRD(H) 10 9 8 7 6 5 4 3 2

The names of select people and places have been changed to honor the privacy of those who have not chosen to live their lives in the public eye. Rest assured, the events depicted in this book have not been changed. They are very real.

CONTENTS

IS YOU OKAY? IS YOU?

"You're going to love my entrance."

I was talking to my mom and my sister. It was just minutes before the start of the 2015 Streamy Awards. I was getting ready to cohost the show and was about to climb to the top of a platform, fifteen feet above the crowd. No one else knew I would be up there.

It was going to be a great night.

I'd made my mom and my sister swear to keep my entrance a secret, to make sure the other six hundred YouTube, Snapchat, and Vine stars in the audience would be totally surprised when I appeared. I'd rehearsed what I was going to do a few times leading up to this moment—twice the day before, and then once in dress rehearsal—so I wasn't scared to take the plunge. I was ready. All I needed was my cue from the director and I'd come sliding down the fireman's pole at the back of the room at the YouTube Space in Los Angeles.

As I stared down at the young, well-dressed crowd milling around below, many of them my friends, I couldn't help but think back to everything that had happened to me in the year leading up to this perfect September night. I had gotten to interview the president of the United States of America (*what?*); I was in a Kevin Hart movie (*so cute*); I was on a Nickelodeon sitcom (*so fun*); I got to fly first class to London to be on a game show (*hiya!*); I went to VidCon (*amazing!!*); I did dozens and dozens of videos to entertain my awesome fans (*obvs*); we did the Third Annual GloZell Festival (*which was in this very building*); my husband, SK, and I had found our surrogate (*blessed*); oh and just a few days earlier, I had been selected to be a cast member on one of my favorite reality competition shows ever (*triple!*).

It felt, unlike any other time in my life, like 2015 had been my year, the Year of GloZell. Not that everyone was talking about me or anything, but nearly everything that I could have hoped for in a given year had happened . . . and gone right. Once up on the platform, fifteen feet in the air and waiting for my cue, I was overwhelmed by a sense of gratitude. This year really had been a dream come true. No, that's not right. That's an understatement. This was like an *Inception* dream come true, one of those dreams you have to write down in order to understand. This was the dream of the dream of my dream come true. And being asked to cohost the Fifth Annual Streamys preshow was the cherry on the dream sundae.

Finally, it was time. I got my cue, grabbed the pole, wrapped my legs around the polished metal, locking them at the ankles, looked down to find my mark, and let gravity do its thing. Wheeeee!

Then, two seconds later, I heard it.

SNAP!

The sound and the sight still haunt me. My right leg was obviously broken, and my foot was bent at a ninety-degree angle from the ankle. It looked like a Tetris puzzle piece— you know, the squiggly one, not the normal L-shaped one. I sat there frozen in place, more out of surprise than pain. I'd never broken anything before (and if you've seen the stuff I do in my videos, that should be as surprising to you as it has been to me). I guess I knew from movies what a broken ankle looked like, but I had no idea how it would feel; fortunately, right there and then, it didn't feel like anything. The adrenaline of the moment had created a delay in my brain between when I saw my ankle and when I felt the pain of what had happened to it. I think I knew that eventually my nerve endings would have to catch up—no one is *that* lucky—

so I was ready when the first jolt of pain shot through my body a couple seconds later.

Nothing prepares you, though. The pain was excruciating, almost blinding, but those two words don't really do it justice. It was like the Hot Pepper Challenge combined with the Wasabi Challenge, marinated in the Hot Sauce Challenge.

Time slowed down. The first thing that came to mind was the reality TV show I was supposed to be on (it involved lots of running and other physical activity). This was supposed to be it—my big break. This is what all the hard work and struggling had been for. As an entertainer who grew up in the era I did, you always hope one day to get the chance to be on the cast of a big show that reaches every home with a television. The idea that millions of people will see your face every week, all season—that's when you know you've made it. And now that big break had been ruined by . . . well . . . my big break.

I know that all might sound odd coming from someone who, until about thirty seconds earlier, was supposed to cohost an online awards show. It might even sound a little ungrateful, if you consider that the six hundred people staring at me right now, or all the awesome fans who subscribe to my YouTube channel, would probably say that I'd already made it. I don't mean to sound unappreciative or inconsiderate at all. I am grateful for every last person who has given me a chance or watched one of my videos.

But there's something you need to understand about me: I'm a little older than the rest of y'all. I grew up *before* the Internet, *before* cell phones, *before* a thousand cable channels. When I was a kid, television wasn't even twenty-four hours—it shut off at midnight and went to a color bars test pattern (you probably don't even know what that is, and honestly, it's too boring to describe). You were lucky if you had five channels, so if you actually appeared on one of them, that meant you were a big deal. And I wanted to be a big deal.

As the people around me finally saw that something was wrong (*hey, that lady who fell from the ceiling isn't getting up*), my mind began to fill with pictures of things that now might never happen: being on TV every week; winning one of the best reality competition shows ever; having an amazing adventure with my best friend; traveling all over the world with other YouTubers; getting my own show.

It was like the next year of my life was playing in my head as a Snapchat story—there one day, gone the next. The Year of GloZell had ended. Not with a bang, but a whimper.

Then, through the whir of mental images and the hum of the crowd, I heard a voice. It wasn't loud, but it was perfectly calm and perfectly clear. It said, "Is you okay?"

If I'm being totally honest, I was pretty out of it from the pain, so I don't know if someone actually said those words or if it was the voice in my head, or maybe even the voice of God, but I swear I heard it. And despite the pain, I listened. Because what it was saying was this:

Stop. Breathe. This is right where you're supposed to be. This is the universe telling you to slow down and appreciate all the things that have happened, and all the people who have come into your life. Everything is going to be okay. This happened for a reason. There are other, bigger chances coming. Just do what you've always done. Keep looking forward, be open to the path, have faith, work hard, don't make any excuses, and everything will work out.

And you want to know the craziest part? It all happened in a flash. From the time I landed at the bottom of the fireman's pole to the time I was on my behind and cool with everything, it was less than a minute. Maybe even thirty seconds.

My friend Colleen Ballinger-Evans (a.k.a. Miranda Sings) was the first person to recognize that I was in a little bit of trouble.

"What can I do?" Colleen said, as I pushed the broken bone in my leg back into place *like a #girlboss!* I learned an important lesson in that moment, by the way. Setting a broken bone hurts much worse than breaking it in the first place.

"Give me a phone," I said.

And then I took a selfie.

When you look at the picture and others from that night as I'm getting wheeled into the ambulance, I don't really look like I'm in a tremendous amount of blinding pain. Colleen looks more uncomfortable than I do. I don't look frightened or panicked, like Katniss Everdeen when Prim is chosen as tribute for District 12. (Girl. Freaked. Out.) No, I was calm. I knew—from listening to the inner voice in that brief moment with myself on the floor—that I was okay.

I spent the rest of the night at the hospital. Let me tell you something about the emergency room: there is an awful lot of waiting for a place with the word *emergency* in its name. Besides a lot of hanging around, the rest of the experience was a blur. I know they set my foot and told me I needed to have surgery. They showed me all the metal plates and screws and staples they were going to use to put my ankle back together, which looked like a tiny Home Depot was going to be inserted into my leg. And I got my own pitcher of water with crushed ice while I waited (yay!).

I hope you never have to be in the hospital for anything, but if you do, then at least you'll get to have the best crushed ice anywhere in the world. It's so perfect, I seriously wonder if they only make it for hospital patients. Like, we know you've had a tough day so here, have the greatest ice water ever. If movie theaters used this stuff in their soda fountains, I would go to the movies every day.

The thing I remember most about what happened after they set my foot was coming home with a deep sense of calm. Any thought about the TV show that was no longer going to happen had melted away. My leg was broken, my ankle was completely shattered (in surgery the following week, the surgeons had to vacuum pieces of bone out), but I wasn't worried at all. I was focused on what was in front of me: finding someone to help me out at home so the responsibility didn't fall to my husband (he still had to go to work). There was other stuff to consider, too: figuring out what we needed to do about our house so that I could roll my wheelchair from room to room easily; coming up with funny ideas for videos in a wheelchair; having my sister, DeOnzell, decorate my wheelchair with green tassels and sparkle paint so I could show all those rappers talking about candy paint and "sittin' on 22s" in their music videos that they ain't got nothin' on me. I'm rollin' two deep on 24s!

Most immediately, I needed to know what time the big Streamy Awards show started on Thursday. I wasn't curious because I was worried about missing it on TV—I was going to DVR it anyway—no, I needed to confirm the time because *I was going;* I had a job to do. Colleen and I were doing the

"Becky" introduction to "Baby Got Back" for a surprise Sir Mix-a-Lot performance during the show. What—you thought I wouldn't go because of one broken ankle? I have two ankles, people. And besides, I had a wheelchair. Anyone tried to stop me, I'd simply roll there myself.

You know that saying "When God closes a door, He opens a window"? Well, it's more than that. For me, He opened the floodgates.

Contrary to all those doubts that rushed through my head at the Streamys preshow when I thought my career had broken apart as quickly as my leg, there's only one word I can use to describe the last three months of 2015: magical.

Just a few days after my injury, I asked to be on the daytime show *The Talk*. I was the second guest; the first guest was Carol Burnett, my idol. She is everything I have ever wanted to be as an entertainer. When I sign off from my videos with a wink and a kiss and an "over and out," it's a throwback to Carol Burnett. I always loved how she tugged her ear to end her show, like a secret message to all her true fans.

Before I went on for my segment, Carol came up to me backstage and introduced herself. *She* introduced herself to *me*. What?! I got a chance to tell her how much she meant to me, and thank her for how much she did for female entertainers. "You're the reason I'm doing this," I said. I didn't realize until sitting down to write this book how many different ways that was true. It was a chance I never thought I'd get in my lifetime.

A couple weeks later, I was invited to fly to New York City to be on *The Today Show* on NBC with Hoda Kotb and Kathie Lee Gifford. It doesn't get much bigger than *The Today Show*. I've watched it every morning for as long as I can remember. And you know what's funny: the day I flew to New York for the show—in my wheelchair, no less—was the exact same day I was supposed to leave to start filming for the reality show. It's weird how those things work out sometimes, isn't it?

The rest of the year was just one thing after another: some of it had been in the works, some of it was opportunities that would not have been possible had I been away doing the filming for the reality show. But none of this compared to what I was about to get to do. I had people—*friends of mine*—asking half seriously, "Should I break my leg to get some of these opportunities?"

First, I was asked to interview Hillary Clinton for Amanda de Cadenet's Lifetime show called *The Conversation*. I couldn't believe it. President Obama to start the year and now Senator,

Secretary of State, and former First Lady Hillary Clinton to end it; are you kidding me?! Hillary is the Beyoncé of politics! We spent an hour together and talked about her roles as a mother and a grandma, topics that are close to my heart because I love both of mine dearly and because my ongoing fertility struggles threatened my chances of being one either. I even bought a styling green pantsuit for the occasion, just for Hillary. She wouldn't admit it, but I know she was *totes jelly.*

Then finally, I was invited to speak at the MAKERS Conference taking place in early 2016. MAKERS is a leadership group that tells the stories of the groundbreaking women of today in order to create the groundbreaking women of tomorrow. The people in this group are leaders, crusaders, fighters, storytellers, revolutionaries. *What did they want with me?* My biggest video of the year was the Kylie Jenner Challenge, where I sucked on a vacuum cleaner hose to make my lips bigger (it works, in case you were wondering). Was I the entertainment, or was MAKERS saying they considered me one of them? I wasn't sure.

Then I saw the theme for the 2016 conference— #TheTimeIsNow—and it all made sense.

By the time 2015 was over, I'd made 120 videos, generating hundreds of millions of views, and I had more than four million subscribers to my YouTube channel. I had met people and been on TV shows that had been important to me throughout my life, been through some very high highs and some very low lows, and come out the other side with an invitation to speak to a group of amazing women to start the new year.

Yes, I was one of them. But I was also different, and I think what made me different was that I don't need to be reminded that the time is now. I have been living that idea, whether I knew it or not, my whole life. And never so much as the three months that followed my accident. Everything that has ever happened to me has helped me to understand that you only have today. There are no excuses. Great friends are important, but knowing yourself is more important. You can do, or be, anything you want if you have faith, if you work hard, learn from your mistakes, and try to stand out.

I realized quickly that the MAKERS Conference was not the only group I was different from. I was (and still am) also different from the six hundred video tastemakers I was supposed to share the night with after I came sliding down that fireman's pole at the Streamys. They were mostly young; I was in my early forties. They grew up with smartphones; I grew up with pay phones. I had been married twice; they were *so* inexperienced. (I don't mean that in a negative way, I just mean in terms of time on this earth.) Some of them were born when I was in college; others were in middle school when I first started posting videos on YouTube. I had an extra generation of life experience on nearly all my friends.

The MAKERS conference took place the first week of February 2016 at a beautiful oceanside resort in Palos Verdes, California, called Terranea. The only thing more beautiful than the hotel were the women inside attending the conference: Gloria Steinem, Abby Wambach, Katie Couric, Caitlyn Jenner, America Ferrera, Bethany Mota (my girl!), Annie Leibovitz, and so many others—all true legends of their craft.

At the opening ceremony, the organizers played an amazing welcome video that featured all these legendary women. The video talked about empowerment and vision and showed the face of every woman scheduled to speak at the conference. All these trailblazing women in the world whom I have looked up to, all in one room—it was unbelievable. Then my face came up on the screen! It was completely surreal. I was one of those people I looked up to! (LOL.)

When I truly considered that some young people looked up to me the way I looked up to Carol Burnett and all the women at this conference, I realized that it didn't make much sense for me to write the kind of book you might expect from a typical YouTuber. Instead, I figured why not take advantage of all these *bonus years* (I'm being kind to myself now) to answer many of the questions—some serious, some silly—that young people often ask me. Why not offer them some hard-earned wisdom and hard-learned advice so they can avoid all the same crazy ups and downs that I had to survive?

So that's what I did.

This book is about all the big lessons in creativity, identity, and adversity that I was fortunately not too stubborn to learn, as well as an account of the moments from my life that led to learning those lessons. These stories are the experiences that made me who I am today, helped me find my home on YouTube, and, most important, taught me that the answer to the question "Is you okay?" can always be YES.

CHAPTER 1

EVERYONE'S A LITTLE DIFF-UH-RENT

Q: Is "GloZell" your real name?

A: Yes. When I was younger I used to tell people my name
was French, because that sounded more refined and
elegant. But really, it is a combination of my parents'
names: Gloria and Ozell. Get it? **GLO**-ria and O-**ZELL**.
It's actually a pretty common practice in the black
community, and I've grown to really love it.

My sister's name is DeOnzell. She's named after the
amazing singer Dionne Warwick (my mom changed the
spelling a little), and my father. It's pretty fitting that she was
named after an awesome diva, because she's an opera
singer now. Takes one to know one, I guess.

I have always been different.

As long as I can remember, even as a little girl growing up in Orlando, Florida—especially then, actually—I felt different. For a start, I never wanted to be what other kids wanted to be when they grew up. Boys wanted to be firefighters or astronauts or football players; girls wanted to be princesses or veterinarians.

I wanted to be the tooth fairy.

I'm deadly serious—I actually went around telling people I wanted to replace the tooth fairy when she retired. I thought that would be the greatest job in the world—and you know what, I still think that, kind of. You get to travel all over the world, you can FLY (*hello?*), you get to go into people's houses and look at all their stuff and you don't get in trouble. Plus you get to leave them some money. You're like a guardian angel with a bank account. That's why everyone loves the tooth fairy. Who wouldn't want that?

When I asked my mother, Gloria, how I could apply to be the next tooth fairy once she got tired of flying all those miles, my mom laughed and dismissed it, but not in the way parents do when they think you're just being a silly kid who doesn't know any better. She did it like she already knew what I was going to be when I grew up, and it didn't involve a pair of wings or dental work.

"Oh no, GloZell, you're going to be a corporate lawyer."

Corporate lawyer? I had no idea what that meant—I was five years old. That didn't matter to my mom, because she was a teacher, and as a teacher, success for her kids meant doing things that involved a lot of school. Doctor, lawyer, engineer, scientist. Why corporate lawyer? I have no idea. Maybe it was because "corporate" means business and business means lots of money? Who knows—when you're young, all that really registers when you hear the words *corporate lawyer* is "not tooth fairy." I thought, *I will never get to fly, and I will never see what toys the neighbor kids have that I don't.* It was a dark day.

Of course, I'm much closer to being a tooth fairy now, as an adult, than I ever was to being a corporate lawyer. It's why I like to wear a green tutu at my public appearances.

Is the green tutu a bit weird for a grown woman? Maybe. If it is, I blame it on my mom—the weirdness, I mean. (The tutu was my choice.) That woman is diff-UH-rent. She's one of my best friends now, but growing up she confused me more than just about anyone else in my life. She could have spoken to my little sister, DeOnzell, and me entirely in Japanese and we would have been less confused.

My mom is one of those people who have a lot of strange ideas about things that often leave you shaking your head.

The stranger the idea, the more right she feels about it. And the more right she feels, of course, the less right she tends to be. What's worse, though—at least when it comes to arguing with her—is that there's always a little kernel of genius inside each of her cray-cray ideas.

A couple years ago, for GloZell Fest she made a bunch of church hats (we call them "church crowns") out of household items—a KFC bucket, a trashcan, a lampshade, a pot and a frying pan, stuff like that. Her plan was to have my YouTube friends model them in an impromptu fashion show. Now I can see my mom's logic with the KFC bucket: to church folks back home, where GloZell Fest was happening to church folks back home in Florida, fried chicken is like the Holy Bird. We eat it so much at church events that *of course* making a formal hat from a KFC bucket would make perfect sense to her. The rest of it, I have no idea, but the KFC bucket? At least I could see the kernel in the Colonel. (And here's the thing: the hats were good. Colleen was one of the models in the fashion show, and I think she actually really liked hers. My YouTube friends *still* ask about those hats. . . .)

See, it's not that my mom is a crazy person; she's very smart, actually, but in unconventional ways. She's like a mash-up of Martha Stewart and Bear Grylls. The thing is, *something happens* between the time a little kernel of genius plants itself in her brain and when it grows into a fully formed idea. That "something" makes the moment of genius blossom into "something that makes no sense," which in turn makes arguing about it with her impossible.

Like I will never forget the time in sixth grade when one of her brilliant ideas left a family friend named Dr. Almont looking like a hockey player. Dr. Almont was a pharmacist like my dad. My dad loved his pharmacy and he cared a lot about his customers, so if he ever had to be away, he would only trust someone he knew well—like Dr. Almont—to take over in his absence. And since Dr. Almont didn't have his own pharmacy anymore (he was older than my dad), he would happily fill in from time to time.

So on the occasion in question, my dad had a week of pharmacy training and certifications to do some place far enough out of town that he called in Dr. Almont.

Nothing really changed at the pharmacy when Dr. Almont filled in for my dad. My mom worked the cash register (when she wasn't giving piano lessons, that is); Dr. Almont filled prescriptions all day, and after school, if DeOnzell and I didn't have choir practice or piano lessons ourselves, we'd come hang out, pretending to do our homework while we watched the TV that sat on the floor behind the counter. If there were a lot of customers, we could watch cartoons or reruns of *Laverne & Shirley*. If it was slow, Dr. Almont and my mom would join us and then they got to choose what we watched since they were the adults.

This particular afternoon we all got to watching *Jeopardy!* Dr. Almont sat in a little chair against the wall, my mom stood leaning against the counter in case any customers walked in, and they went back and forth trying to beat each other to the answer. It seemed like they didn't care if they were right, they just wanted to be first. Dr. Almont would start in before Alex Trebek even finished reading the clue:

Alex: "This sixteenth-century Portuguese explorer—

Dr. Almont: "Who is . . ."

And then his answer would trail off because he had no idea, and he had to reread the clue on the screen that he'd just talked over. This would always give my mom the time she needed to give her answer—which was wrong, like, oh, I don't know, 75 percent of the time?

At one point there was a clue about the royal family and Dr. Almont was silent. No half guesses, no jumping the gun, nothing. The royal wedding of Prince Charles and Princess Diana had taken place only a couple years earlier—everyone had been obsessed with it—so how could he not have at least one name on the tip of his tongue to be wrong about? I looked over, expecting to see him thinking hard—instead, I found him with his eyes rolled back in his head and his whole body shaking to one side. He was foaming at the mouth, his jaw was clenched, and his arms were bowed out in front of him. Imagine Frankenstein trying to hug a tree, and you'll get the picture.

"Mom, Mom, Dr. Almont is having a fit!" I yelled. Back in the day where I come from we called what was happening "having fits." The correct term I learned when I got older was "seizure." Dr. Almont, it turns out, had epilepsy, and sure enough was having an epileptic seizure right there behind the counter of the pharmacy.

My mom started shouting, "It's okay! I know what to do! I know what to do!" Even by sixth grade I knew whenever my mom said, "I know what to do," what she really meant was that she had no idea what to do.

"Don't worry, I know what to do! I know what to do!" she shouted again. "We gotta lay him flat on the ground and put something hard in his mouth so he doesn't bite off his tongue!" She seemed so sure of herself, that's what we did. My sister and I got Dr. Almont flat onto the floor and just stared at him while my mom ran to the back of the store to find something to put in his mouth. Let me tell you, it's very weird to hear the countdown theme music to Final Jeopardy in the background while an old man you've known your whole life shakes on the ground like he's possessed by demons.

I'll take "Please Make This Stop" for $1000, Alex.

My mom ran back after what felt like forever holding a large metal spoon—the kind you see in the pan of scrambled eggs on a breakfast buffet. Now I have no idea why there was a large serving spoon in the back of a pharmacy, but whatever—she got down on the ground holding that thing like it was the Jaws of Life, pinned Dr. Almont's arms down with her knees, and then spent the next two minutes trying to jam the spoon through his clenched teeth. My mom is not the physically strongest lady in the world, but she's no quitter. That spoon was getting in there one way or another.

Dr. Almont came to three or four minutes later. We were all freaked out, but he had been living with epilepsy all these years so he was calmer than us—right up to the point where he ran his tongue over his teeth and looked in the mirror behind the counter. In my mom's panic to get something into his mouth so he wouldn't bite off his tongue, she'd broken off his top two front teeth. He looked like a jack-o'-lantern! Dr. Almont was completely confused, and I'm sure he wanted to be mad, but how could he be? My mom was just trying to do the right thing.

And that was the thing with my mom: she was always kind of right . . . sort of. You are supposed to get someone suffering an epileptic seizure onto their side, and you are supposed to make sure you move any harmful objects away from them. But it's a myth that people having seizures can bite off and swallow their tongue, so you're *not* supposed to put anything in their mouth. Even if they could, you shouldn't use something stronger than teeth to prevent it, let alone try to jam it in there like you're chipping ice off a windshield. In the Old West, when they had to amputate a limb or remove a bullet, they'd give the guy some whiskey and then have him bite down on a leather strap or maybe a broomstick. Not a piece of metal, and certainly not a huge spoon!

But that's my mom. The kernel of the idea is right, and the execution is all sorts of diff-UH-rent.

My mom's tendency toward being different doesn't stop at emergency triage medicine; it includes far less critical things like, oh I don't know, *where she sent my sister and me to school!*

The *idea* was to give us the best education and the most opportunities to succeed. The *execution* involved putting us in a place called the Calvary Presbyterian School. I absolutely loved where I went to school—I'm not trying to hate—I'm just saying that if you've never been to any place with "Presbyterian" in the name, it's usually about as white as the screen or the paper you're reading this on. From kindergarten through eighth grade at Calvary Presbyterian, DeOnzell and I weren't just the only *black* girls, we were the only ones with a *tan*.

Growing up in a big family—my dad was one of eight kids, my mom was one of six—you spend most of your time in the same houses, in the same neighborhoods, going to the same churches, and you don't realize how different things can be (or how different you are) until you're taken out of those familiar places and forced to spend most of your day some place new. I didn't even realize I was black, for instance, until my first day of kindergarten and all the other parents dropped off their children—my new classmates. I was the first one to arrive, which by itself was a miracle since my parents were not prompt people. They always managed to get me to school on time, so I'll give them that, but they never picked me up on time. (It's why I'm so crazy about being on time as an adult.)

So there I was, the first person in class, sitting on my own waiting for school to start. The next person to come into the classroom was a boy named Joey Garratt. I took one look at him and thought, *I'm going to be his friend, because something is wrong with this poor child. His hair is yellow, his eyelashes are yellow, his eyes are blue. Kids are going to have a field day with this sick little boy.* Then a little girl and another little boy came in, and they had the same problems as Joey. *Is everybody in this class sick?* That's really what went through my mind. I wasn't scared, because I knew I wouldn't be able to catch whatever they had. If it were contagious, they wouldn't be allowed in school, right?

Finally, with all of us seated at our little tables and our teacher totally ignoring the fact that she was standing in front of a classroom full of sick children, I realized that they weren't sick. All these little kids my age with their pale skin, light eyes, and straw-colored hair—they weren't sick, they were just white. And I was . . . not.

Ohhh, I'm *the one who's different.*

I know how odd that sounds today, but I also know as an adult thinking back on my first day of grade school in 1977 that those white kids probably felt the same way about me. They didn't hate me, or anything crazy like that, they just didn't know what to make of me. They saw as many black people in their neighborhood as I saw white people in mine. I thought they all had some disease that made their skin lose color and their hair turn to hay. Maybe they thought I got overcooked in my mommy's tummy and that's why I was extra brown, or that my skin was a giant birthmark. I don't know, we didn't talk about it—we were five-year-olds.

Regardless, the differences were very real, and they lasted my entire time at Calvary—all nine years—sometimes for better, sometimes for worse.

On the plus side, I learned that I could make people laugh as early as that kindergarten class, and I think being different had a lot to do with it. Because I acted, sounded, and looked different than all my classmates, the things that I said were naturally just funny to them. And because I could make them laugh, they accepted me. That was huge, and it was something that has stuck with me ever since: that comedy and laughter have the power to break down a lot of barriers.

On the negative side, it couldn't break down their parents' barriers. I was never allowed to go to a lot of my friends' houses. My best friend, Abby, and I spent every possible second of the school day together—up until she switched schools at the end of fourth grade—but we never once went to each other's houses. I guess the amount of time we spent together seemed like enough, so it wasn't an issue, but even if it had been, I was too young to ask why. Our parents knew why, though. My parents knew that her parents would say no if the subject of a visit came up, and her parents knew my parents probably wouldn't ask.

Throughout the rest of my years at Calvary, my other friends' parents wouldn't allow us to have at-home playdates, either. This was the 1970s and early 1980s in the South, you have to remember—black kids and white kids didn't spend a lot of time together outside of school, or off the playing field. Eventually I got old enough to notice it was an issue, but I was still too young to *fully* understand it, so getting turned down hurt my feelings.

My parents, on the other hand, weren't surprised at all. They grew up in the 1950s and 1960s. Forget about going over to a white person's house or having a white friend back then— you weren't even allowed to go to the same restaurants, ride in the same train cars, use the same bathrooms or drinking fountains . . . the list went on and on. Though the racism I faced was a more subtle kind, it was nothing new—same old thing in a different form.

That's why, when I was finally going to have my first sleepover in sixth grade with my friend Patrice, my mother was certain it would never happen. I told her the plan on a Monday: Patrice would come home with us after school that Friday and she'd stay over. We'd go to the water park all day Saturday and she'd sleep over again that night. Then, we'd take her home Sunday before church. I was so excited I talked about it all week on the drive to and from school, and every time I brought it up my mom would try to prepare me for the inevitable:

"You know GloZell, it's okay if she can't make it this weekend."

"I just want you to know that if she can't come, it's not your fault."

"Don't get your hopes up, honey."

"If she's not at school on Friday, don't be sad."

My mom clearly thought that at the last minute, Patrice's parents would have second thoughts, come up with some excuse for why she couldn't stay over at my house, and then they would be spared the embarrassment of their child being seen in the company of a black child. It sounds horrible when you say it out loud, but it was a very real possibility. So when Patrice hopped into the backseat of our car with me after school on Friday, it was like my mom had just seen a ghost. (*C'mon, Mom—Patrice is white, but she's not that white.*)

In retrospect, I wish I hadn't gotten so excited and talkative about the sleepover, because when my mom's cautious, protective side gets triggered, that's when the diff-UH-rent side comes out in full color. Like a sixty-four-count box of Crayola crayons, where all the colors are shades of "Huh?"

This time it came out on Saturday, in the middle of the night, after eight hours at Wet 'n' Wild Orlando.

Saturday at the water park was like most other days in Florida: warm and sunny. We got there early, like you always do when you go fun places as a kid, and made a beeline to claim the best spot for our stuff and maximize the number of rides we could get to with the minimum amount of walking. Adults don't usually give kids a lot of credit, but if they're inspired, kids can be little baby Einsteins when it comes to choreography and planning. (Don't believe me? Go search YouTube for tribute videos to Pharrell Williams's song "Happy" and count the number of videos submitted by groups of eight-year-old girls cracking off synchronized dance moves like they're on an episode of *So You Think You Can Dance*. I hope you have a calculator.)

Patrice and I had on our totally cute sixth-grader swimsuits. They were modest enough that we didn't look like a couple of "those girls," but nevertheless they exposed enough skin that we'd get one of those good tans that always screwed up your pictures when you wore a strapless dress to the Spring Dance. . . . Who am I kidding? I wasn't getting any kind of tan; that was all Patrice. She was a tanning *expert,* as far as I could tell. When I asked her if she needed to put on any of that lotion that white people use when they go to the beach, she said she didn't have any.

"It's okay, I don't burn," Patrice said. This was the mid-1980s, before anyone knew that skin cancer was a big problem or that the sun was almost as bad for you as carbs. My mom and I certainly weren't any help—the only lotion we used was moisturizer for dry skin, or cocoa butter to smell delicious.

Patrice and I spent the next three hours going up and down slides, on inner tubes down the lazy river, splashing in the wave pool. We didn't get out of the water for the first time until a little after one o'clock, when we found my mom camped out at our perfect spot, got some money from her, and headed over to the concession stand to buy lunch. As we stood in line wrapped in our towels debating what to eat, I noticed through Patrice's shivering that she actually wasn't white anymore. She was red, like a crab. Every square inch of her skin that was not covered by bathing suit was a rosy pink color, like a flamingo with a nasty shrimp habit.

"Patrice, are you sure you don't need some sunscreen? You look like a tomato."

"I don't burn, I'm fine. It will turn into a tan overnight." She seemed pretty sure about it, so I let it go. Maybe she doesn't burn—what did I know about getting a tan?—but she sure looked slow roasted to me.

The second half of the day at Wet 'n' Wild was a repeat of the first half. It was nothing but sun and fun . . . and more sun. Everything Patrice and I planned all week was going off without a hitch. Good friends aren't easy to make when you go to a small private school and you're the most obviously different from everyone else, so this sleepover was a big deal for me. It was the best time I'd had in middle school to date.

At normal sleepovers you're up until 2 or 3 A.M., eating sugary snacks that give you the energy to talk for hours about boys, or have a marathon dance party, until you pass out from the sugar crash. We plugged in the disco lamp I won for selling books through the Scholastic Reading Club and danced to the KC & The Sunshine Band "Boogie Shoes" 45 (that's a type of record . . . a record is something we used to listen to on a turntable . . . a turntable is—*OH NEVER MIND!*). With all the sun we soaked up and energy we used during the day, the dance party went from a marathon to a sprint. We were out before my parents went to bed, which is like a cardinal sin of cool sleepovers. You at least have to make it to midnight! Well, in a manner of speaking, we did, because right around midnight, deep in sleep, I was woken up by the sound of soft, pathetic whimpering coming from Patrice's sleeping bag.

She was shivering and moaning and crying all at once. At first I thought she was having a fit like Dr. Almont a few months before, but she was conscious and trying to talk through the pain.

"Mm . . . mm . . . my ski-ii-ii-iin hurtsobad. C-c-can't
mm . . . mmove b-b-but laying o-o-on mm-mm-mmy b-back
hurtsobad!"

Patrice had gone from seared at 11 A.M. to slow roasted at
1 P.M. to well done by midnight. She was like the burnt ends
of a brisket. It was not good; I felt so bad for her. She was
my friend and I hated to see her in so much pain. I had to do
something, so I ran down the hall to my parents' room and
woke them up.

"Patrice's hurt really bad from her sunburn. We need to do
something." I had no idea what that something was, but we
couldn't just leave her there burned in the sleeping bag like
a Hot Pocket.

My parents followed me back into the living room where we'd
set up our sleeping bags in front of the TV, and we all stood
over Patrice while she shook and moaned like a zombie right
before they turn.

"My skin hurts," Patrice said softly.

I turned to my dad. "What should we do?" He was a
pharmacist, surely he'd know. He paused and looked
at Patrice for a second before answering.

"I have no idea." Do they not teach sunburn maintenance at pharmacy school or something? That's when my mom piped in.

"Okay, okay. I know what to do. I know what to do." Uh-oh. Famous last words. "We gotta get the sting out of her skin. Go put her in the bathtub."

Again, to be fair, she had the right idea—that's what aloe vera gel does when you apply it to a sunburn, it removes the sting. But what was my mother—a woman who has never had a sunburn in her entire life—actually planning to do in the bathtub with Patrice?

I think my dad knew this couldn't go anywhere good, because once my mom announced her plan, he turned right around and went back to bed. While my mom disappeared into the kitchen, I unzipped Patrice's sleeping bag and helped her up, being extra careful to make sure absolutely nothing touched her skin.

"C-c-can you c-c-callmymom?" Patrice asked. She sounded like one of those movie characters who thinks they're on a suicide mission and will never see their loved ones again.

"I will," I told her, "but first you need to sit in the bathtub."

Slowly, I got Patrice into the bathroom and lowered her into the tub. She let out a little yelp when her hot skin touched the surface of the tub, but after the initial shock, the coolness of the ceramic seemed to help. Then my mom came in, holding a bath towel and a large plastic bottle of rubbing alcohol.

"This is going to make you feel better," my mom promised her. "Trust me, I know what to do. I know what to do."

If you don't know anything about treating burns, rubbing alcohol is actually a good home remedy for reducing skin irritation and alleviating some of the pain (there's my mom again with a kernel of the right idea). But there's a process to it.

The first thing you do is run the skin under cold water, or take a cool bath, to reduce some of the swelling. Then, you disinfect the burned areas to make sure no bacteria get trapped where there might be blisters. Then, you gently apply the rubbing alcohol to the affected areas with a cotton ball or a soft towel.

My mom decided to skip the first two steps and modify the final one. So she opened the cap on the rubbing alcohol, poured it all over Patrice's body, and then wrapped her up in a bath towel.

You can imagine the problem with that technique. For one, Patrice is not a burrito with extra hot sauce. For two, you're supposed to let the alcohol evaporate. When you immediately wrap her up, you not only trap the heat from the burn that has been trying to escape for the last eight hours, but you trap the alcohol against her skin as well, which dries out and tightens the skin, which HURTS!

Today, more than thirty years later, if I close my eyes and concentrate, I can still hear the screams. My mom—God bless that woman—had just made things worse, despite the best of intentions. I was panicked. We couldn't send Patrice home like this. Her parents might think we're some kind of crazy devil worshippers, exposing their daughter's flesh to the fires of the Orlando sun then baptizing her into our cult with rubbing alcohol in the middle of the night. It sounds crazy, I know. Who would possibly think something like that? You have to understand—this is Florida; weird stuff happens here.

Turns out Mom wasn't finished.

"Okay, okay, I know what to do!" my mom said, quickly leaving the bathroom.

NOOOOOOOOOOOOO!!!!!!

I tried comforting Patrice while my mom went back into her bag of tricks. I offered her something to drink, and suggested running a cold bath, or using an ice pack. Poor Patrice didn't want any of it. She was too disoriented from the pain and the fatigue. She was probably dehydrated, too, now that I think about it. She just sat there in the tub waiting for my mom to return with her new solution.

Want to guess what my mom came into the bathroom with? Take all the time you need, I can wait.

If you guessed a loaf of white bread and a jar of Miracle Whip, you should run out and play the lottery right now because you are a genius.

White bread and Miracle Whip—this was not the kind of miracle either of us were hoping for. Before I could protest—actually, before I could even register what was going on—my mom was plopping globs of mayonnaise onto Patrice's skin with her fingers. She didn't want to use a knife or a spoon—she'd learned her lesson from the Dr. Almont incident earlier that same year—so instead she used the slices of white bread to spread the Miracle Whip into a nice even coat.

My mother had gone from turning my best friend into a burrito to turning her into a sandwich.

If you told me at any point in the next thirty years of my life that this wouldn't be the weirdest thing I'd ever be involved with in a bathtub, I'd have given you all the change in my piggy bank. Fast-forward to my Cereal Challenge video, eating Froot Loops out of a bathtub filled with water and skim milk. You'd be shocked what can find its way into a black bathing suit (twelve million views, for example).

But all that was to come. Back then, as bad as I felt for Patrice in that moment, I felt worse for myself. I was already the only black girl in our class; now I would be the girl whose mom tortures kids by marinating them in the bathtub and then turning them into Lunchables.

Shockingly, Patrice wanted to go home after her Miracle Whip makeover. When you feel as miserable as she looked, all you want is your mother and your own bed. I understood, but I still begged her to stay and to come to church with us in the morning. We could still salvage the weekend, I was sure of it; we could still have fun. Maybe Jesus could help!

Patrice, the saint that she was, gave in.

At church the next morning, Patrice was uncomfortable in more ways than one. Not only was she exhausted and sunburned bright red, but she was also the only white girl in a church full of black people. It was like the setup to a corny joke: What's black and white and red all over? Church with my best friend, the candy cane flamingo.

I'd been going to this church since I was a baby, and to the Presbyterian school church since I was in kindergarten, but having Patrice there with me at my home church was the first time I really recognized that I was in an all-black congregation. This was a different world from the one my classmates belonged to.

The pastor opened our service by saying, "Welcome to the Mt. Olive African Methodist Episcopal Church at 2525 West Church Street. Where Church Street ends and church begins!" He said it every Sunday like it was a new joke. (I don't think Patrice got it, but then, she had other things on her mind, like how she was turning into a giant blister.) We used the same King James Bible and sang from hymnals with many of the same songs as other churches, but nothing sounded the same. "Amazing Grace" was an entirely different song depending on where it was being sung. At school, it was the length of a TV commercial break; at Mt. Olive, it lasted as long as a full TV show. Four minutes barely got you through the intro by the organist. As uncomfortable as she was, I think Patrice got a real taste that day for what my experience at Calvary Presbyterian School was like every day. Watching her try to keep up with the choir, and constantly lose her place, really hammered home both the differences and the similarities in our situation. All the clapping didn't help either—not because she had no rhythm, because the sunburn made each clap hurt.

That poor girl: rubbing alcohol, mayonnaise, white bread, the Holy Spirit. Nothing seemed to help.

Ultimately, I was right about what was going to happen after that weekend. Patrice told some of the kids at school about our sleepover—not in a mean way, just in the way you do when you're in middle school. The story got around and naturally got blown out of proportion, kids teased me about it unmercifully, and no one slept over at my house again. After we graduated at the end of eighth grade, Patrice and I went to different high schools and I never saw her again during my school years.

But can you imagine if this all happened today? One of us would have grabbed our phone and Snapped it or vlogged it. My mom might be one of those frantic people interviewed on the news, like Antoine Dodson ("Hide your kids! Hide your wife!"), or Sweet Brown ("Oh, Lord Jesus, it's a fire! Ain't nobody got time for that!"). It could have kicked off an entire set of memes. Patrice might have been as famous as the Star Wars Kid or the "Leave Britney Alone" guy. It's crazy to think how so much has changed since then, to the point where things get turned into viral videos the second they happen.

A couple of years ago, I did a meet and greet at the very same church in Orlando where I spent my childhood. The place was full of old friends and new fans—it was hard to keep track of everybody. Then a woman walked up to me smiling, carrying an adorable little boy.

It was Patrice. After we hugged and squealed our hellos like we were right back in sixth grade, the first thing she said was, "Remember that time your mom covered me in mayonnaise and white bread?" And we both laughed hysterically.

We talked for a while that day and I learned a lot. While I had tried to put the embarrassing sleepover incident behind me, she'd never forgotten about it . . . or me. I'd stuck in her memory, no matter where life took her. I asked her why she thought that was, but she didn't have an answer.

I think it's because when you're different, you're memorable. If you're a little white girl in Florida, going to a predominately white school, how do you forget the only little black girl in your class? Especially when her mom covered you in rubbing alcohol and mayonnaise in the middle of the night.

That's the great part about being different—it makes you kind of unforgettable. It can be tough early on—trust me, *I understand*—but once you embrace what truly makes you different and unique, it not only allows you to carve out a space for yourself in the world, but it helps you see how much you actually have in common with other people. Sure, I was a different race from Patrice, but we were both from Orlando, we went to the same school, and had the same teacher; we both loved the water park; and we both thought my mom was diff-UH-rent! That's a lot to bond over for two people whose lives went in such different directions. And it helps explain why we were able to pick up right where we left off, there in that old church.

If Patrice taught me anything in that moment, it was this: you should never run away from what makes you different. Don't try to round off all those edges that make you unique in order to fit into a mold that someone else created. The world is full of people trying to fit in. We don't need any more of those people. We need people like you, people who are a little bit different and have something special to say. That is the world I want to live in.

Just remember to use sunscreen.

CHAPTER 2

AGE IS JUST A NUMBER

Q: Is that really your hair? How many weaves do you have?

A: Yes, it really is my hair. I bought it fair and square. It's called a "weave" and I own, let me see . . . one, two, three . . . maybe seventy of them? I have a whole bag full. Which one I wear depends on the occasion or how I'm feeling. Some people think it's funny that I always wear a weave when I'm out in public or I'm doing a video, but hair is like any other accessory. It needs to be convenient, it needs to match your outfit, and it needs to look good when you're putting a bunch of crazy stuff in your mouth!

My dream of becoming an entertainer didn't start as a dream—instead, it developed over time as I tried to cope with all the ups and downs of being at a school where I was the different one.

I got through those first two decades of life in large part thanks to comedy shows like *The Carol Burnett Show* and *The Tonight Show with Johnny Carson*. They made me laugh, they made me happy, and they made me forget the tough parts of being different. Also, watching those shows I learned that being different could bring great benefits—these personalities were not like anyone else, and *they were on TV!* I watched those brilliant comedians do their stuff, and I thought about how they made me feel, and I said to myself: *That's what I want to do—I want to be in front of people and make them smile and be happy.*

But I didn't know the first thing about how to actually become an entertainer. For a start, I had no real concept of the entertainment industry. All I knew was that whatever was happening on those shows happened in California. *The Carol Burnett Show* was "filmed in Hollywood in front of a live studio audience." *The Tonight Show* was coming to me "from lovely downtown Burbank." So that's where I needed to go—I'd figure out the rest once I got there. That's easier said than done when you're young and you live twenty-five hundred miles away on the other side of the country, and more to the point: nobody on these hit TV shows even looks like you.

Fast-forward what feels like a lifetime, and standing up on the platform before the start of the Streamys preshow I had a similar sense, but in reverse. Watching the room full of beautiful YouTubers, Viners, and Snappers mingle, I couldn't help but notice how young they all were. Bright eyed, with smooth skin and perfect muscle tone, some of them were literally half my age. A few of them had been doing videos for literally half their lifetime.

So how did *I* get up here? It felt like only yesterday that I was the young girl in front of the TV, and now all of the sudden I'm *older* than everyone? How does that work?

A couple years ago, my paternal grandmother officially turned one hundred years old. Unofficially, I'm pretty sure she was older than that. We don't know the truth, because she wasn't born in a hospital. *Her* mother gave birth to my grandmother in a shack on the edge of a cotton field in southern Georgia in the 1910s, where stuff like birth certificates and exact dates weren't available to poor black families like theirs. And in any case, their lives were mostly concerned with survival and trying to get by.

The whole age thing didn't seem to bother my grandmother, or at least I don't think it did. I didn't find out until I was a teenager that no one knew exactly how old she was, and you'd think if it were a big deal, someone would have worked it out for her. After we found out that no one knew, my sister and I were always curious what the real number was, but by then all the people who were around when she was born had passed away. My grandmother, for her part, just shrugged whenever we asked. Think about it—how was she supposed to know her age? She wasn't there before she was born. And besides, age is just a number. It didn't matter all that much. That was always her response.

It was a comforting thought as a teenager and then as a college student. This idea that it didn't matter how old you were, that there was still plenty of time to do . . . whatever. I needed that sense of relief the most back then, what with being in a high school that was even smaller (and whiter) than my grade school, and then going to a couple different colleges spread out over several years while I dealt with my dad's health problems (I'll tell you more about that next chapter). The urge to hurry up and spread my wings was strong as I flew through my teenage years, but the forces keeping me in the nest were stronger. There was nothing

I could do about it, and it had the potential to create real friction, but for my grandmother's words.

By the time I got to be the same age as many of my friends down in that Streamys audience, however, my opinions had changed. I thought her saying was nonsense. In my twenties, still in Florida, doing community theater, performing in the church choir, working at random places like Universal Studios, I had become obsessed with the idea that everything changed when you turned thirty—that's when all the fun stops and the exploration ends and you're supposed to get serious. By then you're supposed to know what you're going to do with the rest of your life.

But what if you didn't know? What if you hadn't figured out exactly what you wanted to do with your life by then? Or how to do it? Singing and playing piano with my church choir, doing local music theater, those were all forms of entertainment and ways of being an entertainer; but it didn't feel like enough because I didn't have a clear direction. I mean, I knew I wanted to make people happy, but which people and how? Those were the real questions, and I wasn't sure about their answers. As a result I felt like I was just spinning my wheels there in Florida during my twenties while everyone else was off to the races.

If your twenties are when you're supposed to figure out what you want to do, your thirties are when you're supposed to actually get down to doing it. When I turned thirty, still in Florida, I hadn't done one and I wasn't prepared for the other. Instead, I was worried about what would happen when I turned forty. If you watched TV from back when I was growing up or you listened to "the adults," you'd understand why this was so important—according to them, life was over at forty. That's when you stop being pretty and have an "over the hill" birthday party where people bring black balloons and a cake shaped like a tombstone. If I listened to them, and I didn't quickly figure out all the stuff I was supposed to have learned in my twenties, and then spend the rest of my thirties making it happen, then by forty none of it would matter. My hopes, my dreams, my goals—all of it would be all over.

A lot had changed at the end of my twenties, however. My father passed away. I got married. I met a group of performers—we called our little theater group "Du-Plex"— with similar California dreams to mine. A real direction was starting to make itself known to me. I had every reason to leave the nest now, and the support I needed in case I fell.

Maybe the other old people's lives were on the verge of being over, but I didn't feel old at all. My skin looked great! I had a ton of energy, just like my grandmother, who was still cooking and cleaning, and she was probably ninety at the time. Sixty years older than me. That's a whole other additional lifetime she'd been at it! Suddenly her words started to ring true again.

And that's when I realized: I had my whole life ahead of me. It's not about what I should have learned in my twenties or what I should have done in my thirties, it's about what I can do today and tomorrow and the day after that and the day after that. Your life, your dreams, whatever you're chasing doesn't need to be a hyperfocused vision from the get-go. That story you hear people tell, about how "all I ever wanted to be was a _____," that's not really how the world works. Very few people have that kind of vision, and that is okay.

All I ever wanted to be *wasn't* a YouTuber.

YouTube didn't exist when I was younger. If you traveled back in time to when I was a kid and asked someone about "YouTube," they'd probably think you were talking about the U-shaped pipe under the sink. My original dreams were basic: I just wanted to perform in front of people and make them happy. Having goals like that is a good thing. Feeling a pull in a particular direction is great. I just had to keep reminding myself: *You don't need to have it all figured out.*

When I think about it, that mindset shift is really what reconnected me to those simpler early childhood dreams and kicked me in the behind to get out to Los Angeles. *Get to California, you can figure out the rest once you get there.* The mindset shift also helped me through all the ups and downs over the rest of my thirties in a new city, with new friends, and a new direction. As a result, when forty came and went a couple years ago, I wasn't worried about fifty at all. I felt like I was twenty years old all over again.

I have my whole life ahead of me.

I guess MaDear was right about that whole age thing from the start. That's what we called my grandmother—"MaDear" (pronounced muh-DEAR), as in 'Mother Dear'—because she raised eight kids in the projects, cooked and cleaned for seventy-five-plus years, and honestly that's what she wanted to be called, so that's what we did. You don't talk back or second-guess a strong woman like her. To MaDear, age was just a number because she didn't have much use for it, and she was too busy to think about it even if she had. Raising a big family, corralling a bunch of grandkids, and cleaning "for my white people," as she liked to say, has a way of soaking up all your free time.

The way MaDear lived her life taught me a valuable lesson: thinking about your age, whether you feel too young or too old, is a waste of time. It means you're spending too much time in the past on things you can't change, or too much time in the future on things that might never happen, when there is so much to focus on in the present. When you're not paying attention to the skillet on the stove, that's how you get burned. (Or worse, how you ruin the bacon.)

I moved to Los Angeles when I was thirty-one years old. A lot had changed—in my world, in *the* world—in the twenty years since I'd given up on becoming the tooth fairy, but one thing that remained the same was the basic definition of an entertainer I'd developed from watching Carol Burnett and Johnny Carson.

If you wanted to perform for a lot of people and make them happy, you needed a TV show. But what kind of show? A variety show like Carol Burnett's? Those didn't really exist anymore (they only recently started coming back with Neil Patrick Harris and Jimmy Fallon's version of *The Tonight Show*). A talk show? Those were all older white men who'd been around for decades. I could do a sitcom—in fact, a lot of the shows I loved as a teenager and then in college were sitcoms starring stand-up comics: Red Foxx in *Sanford & Son;* Ellen DeGeneres in *Ellen;* Robin Williams in *Mork & Mindy;*

Roseanne Barr in *Roseanne;* Brett Butler in *Grace Under Fire;* Jerry Seinfeld in *Seinfeld*.

In interviews, the way all these stars described getting a show was pretty straightforward: they performed at all the great comedy clubs around the country for a few years, building an act and a persona, until the right someone saw them do their thing and told them they should have their own show. For most of them, the right someone was usually one of two people: talk-show host Johnny Carson, and his talent coordinator, Jim McCawley. Jim would scout all the comedy clubs in Los Angeles looking for the next big thing, and if he liked you, you got your shot on *The Tonight Show*. If Johnny Carson liked you, if he gave you the "OK" sign or waved you over to the couch, you got your shot to be a star in Hollywood with your own show. Johnny was gone by the time I got to Los Angeles, but Jay Leno was the host then and he was a great stand-up comic too. If he could do it, and these other comics could do it, I thought, so could I.

There was only one problem, at least if you were to ask anyone whom I asked for advice at the time: most people who want to do stand-up comedy start in their early twenties. Some start even younger. Chris Rock, Sarah Silverman, Eddie Murphy—they all started when they were *teenagers*. I was late to the game. I was too old to just be starting.

I didn't care. From 2003 to 2006, well into my early thirties, I started doing stand-up every night. I didn't make any money at the beginning, but that's not really the point when you're first starting out. The goal isn't to get rich, it's to get noticed.

And even more important for me, doing comedy was a way to make people happy—to do for the audience what Carol Burnett did for me. Obviously, doing stand-up didn't result in a TV show of my own, but that didn't matter because I never lost sight of my early, simpler dreams, and I didn't allow tunnel vision to wall me in. Instead, I let myself get pulled in other directions when opportunities presented themselves; opportunities that would never have happened if I didn't give my all to stand-up comedy.

Looking back on it now, it's a minor miracle I stuck with it and survived that period in one piece. Not only had I just moved twenty-five hundred miles across three time zones, but I went from a house near Disneyworld—the "Most Magical Place on Earth"—to an apartment in the Valley next to a freeway and a strip mall with a Goodwill in it. Technically, I was in L.A., but not the L.A. they now show on *Keeping Up with the Kardashians*. It was more like the L.A. they show on gritty cop shows. You know how people sometimes talk about being from "the other side of the tracks"? That's where I lived. I was on the other side of the Hollywood Hills (where all the rich and famous people lived), away from all the famous comedy clubs and all the fun, exciting stuff. I was on the wrong side of the "makin' it" tracks, or so I thought.

Fortunately, striving and surviving out of my comfort zone like that prepared me for the moment I stumbled onto YouTube in my midthirties.

YouTube was still pretty young, then, but pretty quickly it was filling up with really young people posting videos and starting channels. Y'all grew up with most of this technology; it was second nature to you. I, on the other hand, had to learn it from the ground up. What if I had let my lack of technical ability, and the fact that I was fifteen to twenty years older than most of the people on YouTube, stop me from making videos? Imagine where I might be right now?

It works in the other direction too. What if Mark Zuckerberg let himself believe he was too young to start a company based on the website he built when he was twenty years old? What if Taylor Swift or Justin Bieber decided to wait until they were a little older to start recording albums or going on tour? Justin was discovered on YouTube when he was thirteen years old. The guy who discovered him, Scooter Braun, was only twenty-seven years old himself. Today, nobody tells them they're not old enough to do the things they want to do. And if somebody does, my guess is they don't listen too closely. Personally, I think people should stop asking kids what they want to do when they grow up and start asking them, "What do you want to do *now?*"

The point isn't that you have to find something to be really good at, or that you need to have a huge dream. The point is: it's never too early or too late to figure it out. The key is to focus on what is in front of you and live your life in the present so you can take advantage of any opportunity that might come your way.

I have MaDear to thank for that. Not only did she change my outlook on growing up, but the same year I turned forty, when she was ninety-seven . . . ish, was the year she finally stopped cooking. Can you believe that? She was still going strong behind the stove, cooking and cleaning, doing her thing, well into her nineties.

That could be you too, with whatever you decide you want to do, whenever you decide to start doing it. But you gotta do it.

CHAPTER 3

NO EXCUSES

Q: If you were trapped on an island, what five
things would you take with you?

A: A boat for sure. Some electricity, plenty of food, and I
would need Wi-Fi, and my phone. Nobody's trapping
me on an island. And if they try, they sure as heck
aren't going to prevent me from posting videos.

Here's a truth I've found to be . . . well . . . true: this world is a
funny place.

One minute this world can give you everything you've ever
wanted, the next minute it can take it all away, and the whole
time it's giving you every excuse you could ever need to take

the easy road, or just plain quit. When something gets hard—
even something you really love—isn't it so easy to just pull
the covers over your head, curl up in a nice warm ball, and
tell whoever is listening that you're not going to school today,
or work, or the gym, or your friend's house, or that party
everyone has been talking about?

Doing *something* is always harder than doing nothing. Giving
up, or quitting, is the easiest thing in the world, because it
doesn't actually require you to do anything.

I've had so many opportunities in my life to quit, I've lost
count at this point. When I broke my leg, for instance, I could
have stayed laid up on my couch for months and done nothing
while my ankle healed. No one would have blamed me. For a
start, the doctor said I couldn't put any weight on the leg, and
if I *had* to go somewhere, it would have to be in a wheelchair.
That's such a pain! He was pretty much giving me permission
to sit there and do nothing for as long as it took.

There was a part of me that wanted to take him up on his
offer. It's always easier to let things get in your way. But I
didn't let the wheelchair and the broken leg stop me; I would
not give in to that part of myself. And of all the people in my
life, I have one person to thank for that—my father, Ozell. He
never made excuses; he never quit or gave in. No matter what

happened to him, he always lived up to his obligations and did what needed to be done.

Ozell Green grew up very poor.

Being one of eight kids, he didn't get a lot of attention from his parents. His father worked long hours and his mother, MaDear, was busy either cleaning houses for extra money, or trying to keep eight kids clothed and fed, so there wasn't a lot of time for individual affection. Sure, his mother birthed him, and sure, his parents gave him a place to live, but beyond that, they didn't do much of anything for him growing up.

Not that he ever told me that. My father didn't like to talk about those early days—I think he would have been worried it sounded like complaining, and if there was one thing my father never did, it was complain. Instead, I heard about his struggles from other people.

One of my aunts loved to tell about the time MaDear took my father to the grocery store and he made the mistake of asking for a cookie. He was little—I'm not sure he was even old enough to read—but he saw this delicious cookie at the checkout counter and asked if he could have it. MaDear didn't say no; in fact, she didn't say *anything*. She just spanked him. He should have known better than to ask for such an expensive treat.

The cookie cost five cents.

When it wasn't old family stories that gave me some insight into my dad, I would connect the dots myself. For example, when I asked him why he became a pharmacist, he told me about Dr. Palmer.

Dr. Palmer lived across the street from the family when my dad was in high school. As the neighborhood pharmacist—this was before every CVS, Walmart, Walgreens, Costco, and Burger King had a pharmacy in it (okay, maybe not Burger King)—Dr. Palmer was an important man in the community, and he saw potential in my dad. What it was he saw exactly my dad never really knew, but one day Dr. Palmer stopped my father on the sidewalk on his way to school and offered him a job.

"Say, Ozell, why don't you come deliver packages for me?" Dr. Palmer said, like it was the conclusion to a conversation they'd never had. They'd never spoken much at all, in fact—in all their years as neighbors they'd only exchanged the normal hellos. The most my dad ever said to him at one time was "How are you today, sir?"

This was the first time in his life he had ever been singled out this way, and it made him feel very proud. He jumped at the chance and swore he'd never let Dr. Palmer down. Soon, he became one of Dr. Palmer's most reliable employees. He made every delivery on time, he almost never screwed up or missed a day of work, and if he did, he always made it right, no questions asked.

Eventually, Dr. Palmer started encouraging my dad to go to college—something no one in his family had ever done or even considered. "Go to school for pharmacy," Dr. Palmer said, "and by the time you've graduated, I'll be ready to retire and you can take over the pharmacy for me."

Here's this poor, ignored boy given special attention by a respected businessman, giving him an amazing chance to change his future. That's like insane *Annie*-type stuff, right?

There was only one little problem: How on earth was my dad going to pay for college? Dr. Palmer was a wonderful man, but he wasn't Daddy Warbucks. And this was the 1960s— college is expensive enough these days, but at least now there are scholarships and student loans to make it a tiny bit more affordable. If my dad was going to get his education, he was going to have to work to pay for it.

But he wasn't worried. He had a plan—a *ten-year plan*. He'd work half the year, use that money to pay for the next semester of school, then take off the following six months to make more money to go back to school the semester after that. It was one semester on, one semester off, until he finished.

I don't know if there are too many people who would do something like this today—and I don't just mean my dad. I mean my mom, too. She married my dad while he was still in school, working at the pharmacy, and he also had a job as a waiter. She was still a schoolteacher then (she retired when we came along), so you'd assume she had enough sense not to do something so foolish, but I guess at her school they didn't teach you that it's crazy to believe some guy with a plan like my dad's!

A couple years later the plan fell apart. Mr. Palmer passed away suddenly while my dad closed in on the end of his education. Mrs. Palmer, fully aware of her husband's plans, nevertheless decided *not* to give the business to my dad. They had a niece who was getting ready to go to pharmacy school herself, and Mrs. Palmer wanted to keep the business in the family. My dad was really hurt by her decision, but there wasn't much he could do about it. He had no *right* to the business, and it wasn't like there were any legal papers. He had two options: quit to work full-time as a waiter or finish pharmacy school and . . . and then what?

What was he going to do now with all that education? *He* had no idea, but my mom did. She told him that Orlando was a big city, and that our neighborhood could handle a second pharmacy. There was plenty of room for everyone. Smart man that he was, my dad took my mom's advice and opened his own shop. (As luck would have it, he never had to worry about competition from Dr. Palmer's niece. She never actually went to pharmacy school, and Dr. Palmer's business eventually folded.)

I thought a lot about that period of my dad's life while I recuperated from my broken leg. What would I have done in my dad's position? What would you do? What *could* you do? What could anyone do? With a new wife, the easy thing would have been to quit school and work full-time to support his family. I think that's what a lot of people would have chosen. It wouldn't have been the wrong choice—it's brave in its own way. It just would have meant giving up on his dream and on his plan.

If I wasn't Ozell Green's daughter, that might have been my choice if I were in his shoes. Then again, those were a tough pair of shoes to fill. I don't just mean that as a figure of speech either.

Once, my sister and I were looking at old photos from our father's childhood and in one of them he pointed to his feet and said, "Those were the only pair of shoes I ever owned as a boy." He told us how he squished his feet into the same pair of cheap, small, ill-fitting shoes for years and years, from the time he was very young all the way up into high school.

When you grow up poor, your parents can't afford to buy you new clothes and new shoes all the time, so when they do, they have to buy them a couple sizes bigger to give you room to grow into them. MaDear did that for my dad, but she did it pretty early on (he can't remember which grade), and then only once. The problem wasn't that his feet grew too long, like Cinderella's stepsister trying to jam her foot into the glass slipper. If that had been the case, he could have always just cut the toes and the heels of the shoe to make room. No—the problem was that his feet grew too wide. You can only cut the sides of shoes so much before they fall apart, so my dad was forced to endure the constant pressure against his feet as they tried to squeeze their way out.

The result was a tragedy.

Years later, not only were his feet completely messed up, but the shoes had cut off the circulation to his legs so severely that, right around the time I was getting ready to go to college to study musical theater, doctors determined they had to amputate.

His right leg was in worse condition, so they took that one first. In case he took a turn for the worse during the recovery process, I decided to stay in town and go to community college instead of moving two hours away to attend the University of Florida like we'd originally planned. In typical Dad fashion, he handled rehabilitation like a champ, so the following year I made the move up to Gainesville, where the university is located. It wasn't long into the school year, however, when doctors realized they had to amputate the other leg and I moved home for his next recovery. Over the course of about eighteen months, the strongest man I knew lost both of his legs at the knee. How insane and sad is that?

And when folks asked him how he'd lost his legs, his answer was heartbreaking.

"Shoes, man, shoes," my dad would say.

One day I'll get to California, I thought, *just not yet.*

In retrospect, I realize that being there for my dad during his health crisis, instead of pursuing my goals full-steam-ahead, contributed to that twentysomething anxiety I mentioned earlier. I recognize that it slowed me down a little, but I'm okay with that, because I learned a valuable lesson from the one person it *didn't* slow down: my dad.

Dad didn't quit working, and he didn't use being unable to walk on two feet as an excuse for not getting things done. I've seen him strap shoes to his knees and climb up a six-foot ladder. He once picked me up off the couch from his knees and carried me when I didn't feel well. I'm a tall woman, so trust me, that's not easy.

After my accident, when people complimented me or told me how amazed they were that I was getting on planes and making TV appearances and doing collabs, I looked at my dad's example and I thought, *A broken leg is supposed to stop me from what I need to do? I still have things I want to get done. What excuse do I have not to do them? None.*

My dad started with nothing, just like his seven brothers and sisters. He built a successful pharmacy business on his own and raised two successful daughters. To me, that proves that no matter what comes your way, or where you come from, you can choose to make something of yourself and for yourself, or you can choose not to. There are no excuses.

Of all the lessons my father taught me, this is the one I have carried closest to my heart as an adult. I even wrote a poem

about it and leaned on it for support when I finally moved out
to Los Angeles. Lord knows, I was going to need it.

I SAID NO EXCUSES

I said no excuses!
Yes! I am talking to you,
Go on and do what you are assigned to do
Get all your equipment and don't be late,
come ready to work, get in the gate.

I said no excuses!
You know I can't hear,
My dog ate my homework,
I'll do better next year.

I said no excuses!
Use your imagination,
there's no variation on procrastination.
Never do tomorrow what you can do today,
Do your job correctly and do it right away.

I said no excuses!
It's time now to shine,
Let anything negative step behind.
Settle for nothing but the best,
You only live once so don't take less.

You have all the facts,

So it's conclusive,

I SAID NO EXCUSES!

If you've never been to Los Angeles, let me just tell you, it's a weird place—Hollyweird.

For starters, there isn't really *one* Los Angeles. There are like *seven* of them, and it's hard at first to figure out which one of them has your kind of people in it. Each one has its own character that, when combined with all the others, makes L.A. the most interesting place I've ever lived.

The easiest way to get comfortable in L.A.—or any new city for that matter—is to move there with someone you know, so you're not alone as you discover new places and learn your way around. I moved out to L.A. in 2003 with my husband Tike and our two pets—a dog and a cat. We'd been married three years when we made the jump across the country. Tike shared my dream of making it in Hollywood. I was the singer and comedian who wanted to make millions of people laugh on my own show; he was the doctor interested in acting. We were a power couple in the making, like Brangelina or Kimye without as catchy a name. GloKe? TiZell?

Because life is not a fairy tale—or anything like what you see in movies—we experienced difficulties from the very beginning.

Tike's desire to be an actor meant he had to find an acting coach, take classes, get headshots taken, go out on tons of auditions, the whole nine yards. It is not an easy path to pursue considering the amount of competition, and the fact that having talent wasn't going to be enough. Nearly every good-looking waiter, smoothie bar cashier, personal trainer, or department store clerk you run into in Los Angeles has some level of talent and is working hard to make it. Many are working one full-time job (their day job) to afford the chance at a second full-time job (their dream job). That's what it's like trying to break into acting in Los Angeles. Even if you're one in a million, in an area with thirteen million people that means there are a dozen other people just like you.

If that wasn't already hard enough, acting classes and auditions happen during the day, whereas stand-up comedy, which I was doing, happens late at night. This meant when my husband was out, I was home sleeping, and when I was out, he was home sleeping. We barely saw each other for weeks at a time, and when we did manage to share a meal together, it would almost always end in silence because I would tell him about my gigs, and he would make excuses for all the jobs he didn't get. The pressure on our relationship began to take its toll pretty quickly.

Then things got even tougher. Barely six months after we'd made it to California, Tike's father died tragically when he rolled his car in a ditch less than a mile from his home in suburban Detroit. It was sad and unexpected and a shock to everyone, not just because all car accidents are that way but because my father-in-law was such a strong guy. He'd worked hard his whole life, yet he'd been on kidney dialysis for nearly twenty years! People like him aren't supposed to go in such random ways like that.

Tike's dad's funeral was scheduled for a Monday in Michigan—he and my mother-in-law lived there, along with most of her side of the family. Tike and I flew in over the weekend and stayed with his mother as she dealt with final details and condolence visits from neighbors and friends. The service itself was lovely. There were touching tributes, meaningful readings from the Bible, and I played the piano and sang a song.

This was a rare thing for me, and I took a lot of pride in it, because my husband's family didn't really like me. I was a musical theater major; Tike had studied science and gotten his doctorate. I was a comedy actress wannabe, he was a *doctor*. Those weren't distinctions I made—I just thought he was a nice, caring man—but it didn't matter. His family had decided long before we got married that I wasn't good enough for him. Still, by being there all weekend and performing at the funeral it felt like I had redeemed myself (from what I wasn't sure). Either way, I was finally in their good graces.

That lasted about three hours.

When the funeral and the wake were over, we all went back to my mother-in-law's house. We were chatting and reminiscing like you do after these things when something amazing happened. Tike's mother started talking about funeral plans for her late husband, like we hadn't just attended it. She talked about what kind of music she wanted, where they should get the flowers, who should sit where in the church. It was as though the funeral hadn't happened. I dismissed it as the shock of sudden grief—she was clearly out of it, having just come from burying her husband and filling up on fried funeral food.

I found a moment when she was distracted and pulled Tike into the kitchen to ask him if his mother was okay.

"She's fine," he said, "she's talking about the other funeral this weekend in Mississippi."

Other funeral? MISSISSIPPI?

It turns out they were going to have a second funeral in Mississippi all along, since that's where his father grew up and was where a lot of *his* family still lived. It just so happened that my husband never bothered to tell me about it.

This was a problem.

From the minute we got the news that my father-in-law had passed away, the plan was that I was going to fly to Michigan with Tike for the funeral, perform the song they asked me to do, be there for him during his tough time, and then travel on to Florida where, the following weekend, I was booked to do a show. The venue had already sold lots of tickets, *my* family was planning to attend, and more important, I'd signed a contract. I'd given my word. Now, I'm just finding out, there would be a second funeral on the same day that I'm scheduled to perform some six hundred miles away? With all the ups and downs I'd been through at this stage of my life, it was only fitting that a dead man created the first scheduling conflict in my young career!

I didn't know what to do.

On the one hand I felt like I had fulfilled my obligation to my in-laws and I had been there for my husband like a good wife is supposed to be. It wasn't my fault that I didn't know they scheduled two funerals—and anyway, *who does that?* Who gives a loved one a proper funeral and then says, "Hey, let's

take this show on the road"? On the other hand, if it meant
that much to Tike, I would cancel the show and deal with the
consequences. We talked it over in my mother-in-law's kitchen
and came to a decision.

I left for Florida the next morning.

The decision deeply upset my mother-in-law, but Tike
promised that he would take care of the second funeral (and
his mother) while I did my show. We were apart for that
whole week—him with his family in Mississippi, me with
mine in Florida, before we both headed back to California
to pick up where we'd left off. I got back to L.A. first, and
Tike arrived a couple days later, with a suitcase full of dirty
laundry . . .

. . . and a handful of divorce papers.

The suitcase could have been filled with bricks and I don't
think it would have hit me any harder. I mean, where'd he
even get the papers? This was pre–Legal Zoom—how did he
have time to find a lawyer? We'd been married three years
and hadn't experienced any issues to that point, beyond not
seeing each other much as we tried to make it in Hollywood,
so as shocked as I was, I tried to understand. He'd just
tragically lost his father and was now about to lose his wife.
I thought maybe the divorce papers were just a side effect
of depression. I told him I'd wait until the end of the month

before signing the papers, hoping that perhaps some sanity would find its way in.

It never did.

Within three weeks he'd paid next month's rent, moved out, and completely disengaged. This is just me speculating, but throughout that whole week when we were apart, I am pretty sure the constant drumbeat of his mother's disapproval finally wore him down. I am one hundred percent sure he let his mother believe the decision to skip the second funeral was all me, and that he had nothing to do with it. He'd made a string of excuses for his acting career from almost the very beginning, so honestly it only made sense that he make excuses for himself when it came to our relationship. His excuses cost him on both fronts: he quit on his dream, and he bailed on our marriage.

Ladies, if you get married, know who your competition is: it's not other women, it's your mother-in-law. And guess what, you won't win. If you can find a man who makes you happy, and he doesn't have a relationship with his mother, snap him up! (I'm joking, obviously, but only kind of.) To Tike's mother, there could only be one winner for his affection and it was going to be her. She was right. She was clearly the only winner in this mess.

If life wasn't a fairy tale before, well, I don't know the name for what it became. Because now I faced a type of adversity I had never experienced before.

When Dr. Palmer passed away, it changed everything for my dad. It could have thrown his entire plan into disarray if he'd let it. He could have thrown up his hands and quit. He was the opposite of Tike in that way—he made no excuses and got down to work. So that's what I would do, too.

I immediately went into survival mode. Stand-up wasn't paying anything, and California is expensive, so I had to figure out how on earth I was going to live here. I knew I wasn't going to go back to Florida with less than I came to California with—when I left, I had a husband, a dog, and a cat (which Tike took)—and I certainly couldn't go back with nothing at all.

Fortunately, I always knew deep in my heart, for as long as I could remember, that if I could just get to California, I would always be able to figure something out. I took a page right out of my dad's book: I would get two jobs to pay for my dreams. So I worked at a Sylvan learning center and an all-women's gym during the day, which paid the rent while I did stand-up at night.

You might think a situation like this would cause me to scale back my stand-up. *GloZell, you're divorced and you'll probably need to move out soon, maybe you should take a step back and regroup?* No—it inspired me to do the opposite. I dove in headfirst. To quote Sheryl Sandberg, this was one of those moments where a lady has to *lean in*.

I went into Hollywood and hit the clubs every night. Monday was The Improv on Melrose. Tuesday was Ha Ha Café in North Hollywood. Wednesday was The Comedy Store on Sunset. Thursday was The Laugh Factory a couple blocks down from The Comedy Store; and then the weekend was a free-for-all. This is what the greats did to get their TV shows, so this is what I was going to do.

The next three years were the toughest of my career, but I'm positive I wouldn't be where I am today if I hadn't gone through them. I had taken complete responsibility for my life and my career after Tike left, and it made all the difference. I learned who I was and who I wasn't during those years, and I figured out what I *really* wanted. I met new people and made new relationships that would propel me into the next phase of my career. And I know that if I'd spent all my time putting blame on other people for my situation, if I'd made excuses for myself, none of that would have happened.

That's the dangerous part about excuses—they are so much easier than the hard work you have to put in to be successful in whatever you want to do. It doesn't matter what it is: music, comedy, tennis, drawing, making videos, being a good friend. As Tike found out, talent isn't enough. You have to be willing to put in the work no matter what comes your way, whether it's a broken leg or no legs at all. Now I can't promise you that if you do the work, everything will work out. But I can guarantee that if you don't do the work, nothing will work out.

So please, ladies and gentlemen, boys and girls, friends and family, neighbors and pets, do not ever, ever, ever, ever let circumstances stand in the way of something you want to do or something that needs to get done. Don't make excuses. If it's hard, don't hide under the blankets. Yank them back and get down to it. You'll be shocked how much you can accomplish when you approach problems that way. You'll surprise yourself with how easy it becomes and how good you are at it. And you'll feel better about yourself as a result.

There is just no excuse for not working as hard as you can to be or do everything you've ever dreamed of. You can "explain" until you're blue in the face, but like my dad would say if he were alive today, you still won't have a leg to stand on.

CHAPTER 4

ALWAYS HAVE FAITH

Q: Whatever is to the left of you is your weapon
during the zombie apocalypse. What is it?

A: A half-eaten bag of cashews. Hopefully zombies
have a nut allergy, because I can't run for jack after
my ankle surgery. That thing is held together with
hope and a prayer.

When Tike and I got married in 2000, we moved into a new
house and joined a church in a suburb of Orlando.

If you are the churchgoing type, and you're still young, let
me just tell you that you still have a lot to look forward
to. There's something unique and powerful about joining

a church together as a newly married couple. Marriage is about starting a new life as a unit, where you make decisions together in each other's best interests.

The problem is, no one really tells you how to go about actually being married.

You might have a big ceremony, and you might hold hands and look into each other's eyes while you promise to have faith in each other, then all your friends might throw rice at you as you run to the car. But when they close the limo door behind you, then it's just the two of you looking at each other like, "Okay, what now?"

That's where a good church comes in. When a church is a nurturing community, the whole congregation gets behind you. When you are struggling, they provide support that oftentimes becomes the foundation for the life you're building together. When you are having doubts, they will lift you up. That's the ideal situation, anyway. Sometimes, it doesn't quite work out like that.

———————

The church Tike and I joined was deeply invested in us, so we grew to be invested in them. We got to know and like the pastor, as well as many members of the congregation.

We tried to go to services as regularly as possible, not just in service to our faith but in service to those growing relationships as well.

It was comforting, though it wasn't always smooth sailing.

One night, the church leaders invited a special guest to lead us in prayer. I forget her name, so I'll call her Sheila, but she called herself a prophetess. A prophetess is basically a combination of a priest and a fortune-teller—someone who channels the Holy Spirit *and* will tell you your future.

Sheila, the prophetess, reminded me of one of those old-school preachers who would lay hands on you and baptize you in a river. The congregation was very excited about having her in our house of worship, so everyone wore their *best* Sunday-best, arrived extraearly, and staked out prime pew seating. The pastor welcomed everyone, did a quick sermon like an opening act before a concert, then handed over the pulpit to the headliner.

When Sheila took the stage, the entire congregation got quiet—it was clear they knew what was coming. That woman could preach her tail off! I was amazed at what I was seeing. The "Hallelujahs" and "Amens" were flying back and forth between Sheila and fellow church members. It was inspiring. She had a ton of passion, and she had even more oxygen. Her sermon was long, like weekend lines at Disneyworld long.

Despite the emotion swirling around the room, thirty or forty minutes in, I got bored. I have a strong work ethic, but I don't have the best attention span, so I dug out a pen from my purse and started filling in the holes in all the *O*'s, *P*'s, *D*'s, and *B*'s in the program. When that was done, I flipped the program over and played tic-tac-toe with myself. It didn't take long before I was completely zoned out and Sheila's words became background noise. I figured nobody would notice since the place was packed and everyone was listening so intently.

Silly, silly GloZell.

At some point mid cat's game, Sheila started calling people up to the front. You might think because of my reputation as an extrovert that I'd gravitate toward situations like this. Nope—this was my worst nightmare. I always get called on in situations like this. It's the curse of being different, I guess. You're easy to spot. Don't get me wrong, I love being up on a stage in front of people, but only when I choose to be, not when someone else decides, and especially when I have no idea what that person has been saying!

Sure enough, Sheila starts pointing at me. I wanted to melt into the pew or hide behind the church crown on the lady in front of me, but it was no use. When a prophetess handpicks you from the crowd, you aren't just chosen . . . you're *Chosen*.

Eventually, a dozen of us found ourselves on the altar, all lined up in a row. I was in the middle. I had no idea what was coming, though the others seemed to know because they were vibrating with excitement. Sheila started with the woman at the far end, to my left. Her words started as a whisper—part chant, part prayer—and then built in volume and speed until she boomed:

IN THE NAME OF JESUS!

And then Sheila hit the woman on the head, sending her fainting to the ground, seized by the Holy Spirit.

The congregation gasped and shouted out their "Amens!" The woman who had been hit on the head rolled around for a few seconds and moaned something I couldn't quite hear. (She reminded me of Dr. Almont when he had his epileptic fit, actually.) When the woman stopped moaning, an assistant helped her to her feet, and then Sheila moved down the line. She performed the same ritual each time—quiet chanting, rising to a huge "In the Name of Jesus!," then the smack on the head, and the collapse, and the rolling around.

All these people seemed to be in a total out-of-body state—it was clearly a very real experience to them. They seemed to all be in the moment—problem was, I wasn't. I felt like everyone else had been hypnotized but Sheila's spell hadn't worked on me, and now the hypnotist was expecting me to do weird stuff too. I started to worry: *I'm not going to fall out. I don't think I'm going to fall out. Am I going to fall out? What if I don't fall out?*

A big part of me doubted the whole thing.

The churches I attended growing up offered much more of the average church experience. The pastors were much more, well, pastorlike. This was my first experience with something like this call-and-response sermon, or with someone like Sheila. I understood the words coming out of Sheila's mouth individually—they were words borrowed from the English language—but the way she put them together was totally bizarre. I was twenty-eight years old, a new wife, a fairly new parishioner, and I could not be any less prepared for this if you dropped me onto that altar from space.

In addition, I knew that the service was being filmed, and I knew from how people were talking about Sheila before the service started that she was a big deal, and people wanted to impress her. I'm sure some of the people up there with me were feeling it, but I figured everyone else just kind of let it happen because they didn't want to be the ones to make things awkward.

As Sheila got closer, I fell into a near panic. What was I going to do? I wasn't feeling anything, and if she didn't bring the feeling with her, I was going to have to pretend. I did not

want to embarrass her if I didn't feel the Spirit. And if she
was as big a deal as these other ladies made her out to be,
a tiny part of me wanted to make sure I didn't get smited. I
actually thought to myself, *I wouldn't want to make God look
ridiculous here by ruining the program.* What's that saying:
fake it till you make it? That's how I felt right then.

Finally, Sheila gets to me and I am in a full flop sweat. If
you didn't know any better, from looking at me it might
have seemed like I was on the verge of being overcome. *I
wish.* Sheila takes my hand, looks me in the eye, and starts
her prayer-chant. I'm not feeling a thing. *Oh boy, I'm gonna
have to go down.* Her voice starts to rise and quicken. *Here it
comes.* She booms:

IN THE NAME OF JESUS!

Based on everyone else's reaction before me, I was expecting
her to high-five my forehead like a *Family Feud* buzzer
and send me reeling backward. Instead, she just tapped it,
like she was Vanna White and my forehead was a *Wheel of
Fortune* tile. Now, I'm a performer, so I'm all about selling the
moment, but one of the first things they teach you in acting
classes is the importance of making scenes feel real. In that
moment, falling to the ground didn't make sense—there
wasn't enough force behind her tap. Instead, I wobbled and
let my knees buckle, and I made a noise that sounded like a

ghost in a kindergarten haunted house. It was *not* convincing. And Sheila was not impressed. She went through the chant with me a second time and boomed once more:

IN THE NAME OF JESUS!

This second time, she popped me with a little bit more force, and I fell out in a way that I considered to be believable. It wasn't real—though I would have liked it to be, just to know what it felt like—but it looked real, and at this point that was all I was worried about. There was only one small detail I hadn't figured out: How long was I supposed to stay down there? Everyone else seemed to have a sense of when it was right to sit up and get helped to their feet by Sheila's assistant. But not me—I had no idea. The last thing I wanted to do was get up too soon. They might know I was faking if I did that. So I went the other way. I stayed down . . . for the rest of the sermon!

Sheila sent five other people falling out after me, and I stayed on the ground, captured in the Holy Spirit, the entire time. It was a little ridiculous. Finally people were, like, "Okay, GloZell, the service is over, you can get up now."

Have you ever been in one of those situations so crazy that after it's all over you have trouble describing it to people? Well, this was one of those situations for me. I had managed to make the whole thing awkward, just in the opposite direction from how I originally feared. A stranger had hit me in the head twice and then I faked passing out in front of my new husband and the congregation out of fear that *they might judge me!*

This is a pretty good lesson about why "just going along" with what everyone else is doing is rarely a good idea. Faking it for other people's sake usually makes stuff worse.

Faith is important to me—but it has to be *true* faith. No matter which churches I've attended, no matter how supportive their congregations have been of me and my family (and believe me, we've needed it), it was always my faith that was my bedrock. People like Sheila the Prophetess shake that belief a little and bring the skeptical part of my personality to the surface because it doesn't feel like it's connected to a deeper faith—it feels like a performance. When you really want to believe, it hurts that much more to be deceived.

If my skeptical side was reading this book, you know what she might say after reading the first few chapters?

Yeah, all that's easy for you to say. It worked out for YOU. But what about me?

It's easy to say that it's okay to be different, that it doesn't matter when you start, that if you don't make excuses and work hard on what needs to be done, everything will work out in the end.

But how? How do you do all that? I had no answers to those questions for a long time. I'm still not sure I do, if I'm being perfectly honest—I only know how *I* got to where I am today.

And for me, it really did start with faith.

My whole life I've been a Believer. I've had a personal relationship with Him. I've known the Word. I've had Faith. Actually, it *started* with Faith with a capital *F* (as in my religion), and then, as I got older and wiser, it turned into faith with a lowercase *f* (as in belief). It was when I found *that* faith that things really started to change.

I've been going to church regularly since I was a baby.

Churchgoing started with my parents, who were fairly religious and made sure my sister and I knew the Word. Being a music teacher, my mom taught me to play the piano and sing before I learned how to read, and the best place to develop that talent when you were as young as me was at church, so I sang in the choir at my mom's church, and at my school church.

When I got to high school, beyond being fairly religious, my parents also got fairly protective. They were always worried that the bad kids in the neighborhood would do something to us, or convince DeOnzell and me to join them in acting out, like we lived inside one of those antidrugs public service announcements. What this meant for us in practice was that if we ever wanted to do anything after school besides sit around the house and watch TV, it would have to involve the church. Church was where the good kids and the good influences were. (Plus they had snacks.) What more could you ask for as a parent? God was basically our babysitter, and my mom didn't even have to get in the car—the church would pick us up and drop us off, too.

Like any high school girl, I wanted to get out of the house as much as I could. If church was the only way that was going to happen, then so be it—I would take advantage. So I signed up to sing and play piano for any congregation that had room for me. Besides playing at my mom's church and school, I played piano in the youth choir, and I found other congregations with good music programs, too. That's another reason to go to a good church—those church members taught me more about music and performing and collaborating with others than anyone else. And they did it out of the goodness of their hearts.

One of those places that helped me learn how to perform was the youth choir at a traditional Methodist church run by a man named Pastor Davis. His church was the first time I felt a real connection—not only with God, but also with the people and the pastor, and *myself.*

I think what connected me to that church was the fact that I had found it on my own and decided to join it myself. I was a baby when I was baptized, so I didn't have the chance to make that decision, and then had no say in where my mom went to church or where I went to grade school. Those places of worship were chosen for me. Pastor Davis's church was *mine.*

Pastor Davis was old school. The church had a shop where girls learned how to sew and the boys learned woodworking or how to fix cars. I don't think you could get away with such strict gender roles today, but back in the day, Pastor Davis didn't care—he just wanted to give his young people skills.

Pastor Davis took to me right away. He loved my hard work and strong spirit so much he even wanted me to marry his son, Calvin.

Well, that's not true exactly—it's not that *he* wanted me to marry Calvin, it was that *He* did. "God told me you were going to marry my son," Pastor Davis told me one day while I was still in high school. I was a good daughter, a good

student, and a good Christian—if God told Pastor Davis that
I was going to marry his son, He must also have told him that
everyone thought Calvin was a jerk, right? I wouldn't believe
it, if He didn't tell Pastor Davis that, too. I sure couldn't
believe it—the God I knew didn't test people like this! In
retrospect, should I have questioned Pastor Davis's judgment
a little right then? Possibly. But I was young, and this was
Pastor Davis, and I was dedicated to his church.

I ended up playing for Pastor Davis's youth choir for several
years—through the end of high school, while I went to
community college and took care of my dad, then my first
three years at UF. I'd come home every weekend most times
just to play. I probably should have found a church up at the
University of Florida, to have a chance at a more traditional
college experience, but I didn't want to leave Pastor Davis's
congregation, and they didn't want me to leave either. I was
a young person playing for their young people. I was a role
model for them. The church leaders respected me and were
proud of me. I was somebody there.

My experience at Pastor Davis's church was the first time
I can remember feeling within me a sense of something
greater than myself. Having a talent was good for my self-
esteem, especially when I was young (and different), but there
are limits to talent for its own sake. If it doesn't take you
anywhere, what's the point? When you attach that talent to

something bigger, though, that's when mountains really start to move. For me, playing at that church transformed my *crazy dream* of becoming an entertainer into *a purpose* that was completely attainable. I'd been doing it to packed pews for more than five years. Why couldn't I do it to full theaters or live studio audiences?

My Faith, I realize now, had helped me find *faith* . . . in myself. It was a great feeling.

––––––––––––––––––

Faith isn't a simple, uncomplicated thing, though. There's a tricky part to it that they don't teach you about in school or in church, and it's this: Faith can make you lazy. Faith can be so comfortable, like a warm blanket, that it lulls you to sleep; so grounding, it cements you in place; so self-affirming, it feels as natural as breathing. Faith makes it easy to go with the flow, without any worries about where the flow is going or whether you want to go that way.

This will probably sound as crazy to read as it was to write, but I first learned all that about faith by wearing pants.

In the summer before my senior year at UF, I had slipped comfortably into my routine back at home—helping my dad, playing with the youth choir—and without thinking, one

day I wore pants to choir practice. You would have thought
I walked into the church wearing no pants at all. One of the
older women in the congregation immediately grabbed me by
the elbow and pulled me aside.

"Young lady, you are not allowed to wear pants in church,"
the older lady told me. "Women shouldn't wear pants."

Not allowed? Pants? Really?

After choir practice, Pastor Davis called me into his office.
The walls were covered in portraits of Jesus and the Apostles.
On his desk was a well-worn Bible.

"GloZell, I want you to read something," Pastor Davis said.
He turned the Bible around and slid it in front of me.
"Deuteronomy 22:5."

I found the verse and recited it as Pastor Davis nodded along
in agreement.

"A woman shall not wear that which pertaineth unto a man,
neither shall a man put on a woman's garment; for whosoever
doeth these things is an abomination unto Jehovah thy God."

When I was finished reading, I just sat there. Pastor Davis
looked at me, looked at my pants, looked at the Bible, then
looked back at me again. It was like he was trying to connect
the dots for me with his eyes. But I didn't need any help; I

knew what he was getting at. I guess he still wanted to make sure, because then he said, "Anyone who is going to marry my son needs to know the rules," like he was letting me peek at the answer key in the teacher's manual to the textbook on Faith.

What is wrong with these people? I thought. *We're talking about pants. Are they crazy? But wait, this is in the Bible, this is the Word, it can't be* that *crazy. Does this mean there's something wrong with* me?

Today, especially in America, it might be hard to grasp the notion that a girl wearing pants could create this much turmoil. I mean, there is a whole series of books dedicated to a magical pair of jeans that fit an entire *sisterhood* of girls! How bad could pants really be? What you need to understand is this was a different time, and a different place, and issues like this were very real. They are issues that women in other parts of the world still struggle against, actually.

I truly was conflicted as I sat silently across from Pastor Davis, thinking about everything I had learned in church since I was a child, and everything I had learned over the previous three years at UF. I had been studying the history of costume and fashion while getting my bachelor's of fine arts in musical theater, so I knew a few things about clothes. For example, did you know high heels were first designed for fancy, aristocrat *men*? Then I thought about burly Scottish men in kilts, and bearded Arab men in thawbs (those long, floor-length robes). Finally, I looked around Pastor Davis's office at framed pictures of all these holy men . . . all of them wearing liturgical garments, a.k.a., dresses.

Nobody would ever say a Scotsman in a kilt isn't manly—and certainly not to his face. No one would call an Arab man in a thawb a woman. And let's not even get started with Jesus or the Apostles, walking around the Holy Land in robes.

I wasn't going to debate Pastor Davis, though. Not only was I a little unsure of my arguments back then, but pastors are like fathers—arguing with them is useless. You're better off just nodding respectfully, taking from them what makes sense to you, and then ignoring the rest. Plus, I already knew what Pastor Davis would say: *That's different—Jesus lived thousands of years ago. Times have changed.*

And that would have been exactly my point! It was 1996. Bill Clinton was the president. My girl Hillary was the First Lady—the queen of pantsuits! Everyone in the congregation probably voted for Bill Clinton. Were these people trying to tell me that it was okay to vote for Bill, but don't you dare dress like his wife? It made no sense to me.

My conversation with Pastor Davis had a deep effect on me. Doubt started seeping in—doubts about myself, and doubts about the church. Times had changed, styles had changed, *I had changed,* even many biblical interpretations had changed. The only people who didn't seem to get the memo were Pastor Davis and some of the ladies in the congregation.

And so, in my last year at UF, I decided to stop going to Pastor Davis's church altogether. It didn't feel right to worship there anymore.

This made a lot of people very unhappy—mostly for their own selfish reasons related to the choir, I would say—but I realized I had to start thinking on my own and questioning what I had been taking for granted, or else the doubts would continue to grow. I was still a Believer, but I didn't believe what *they* believed. Their Word was not the Word I had come to know.

Leaving that church was a very scary thing to do, at least at first. The faith I found in that church was my foundation, the first foundation I chose for myself. Leaving it would be like flying without a net. What if I was wrong? What if I misstepped? If I fell, it would be a long way down.

What made the decision easier to bear was the uncomfortable fact that my Faith had started to shake the faith I was building in myself, right at the time I was beginning to recognize how important *both* were to me. I couldn't let one jeopardize the other, not if the conflict was going to make me feel this way, which was horrible.

I know a lot of people don't have the same kind of religious faith I do, and that's totally great. When I talk about Faith with a capital *F*, I'm not really referring to religion, anyway. What I'm talking about is a belief in something bigger than yourself. It can be God, of course, but it can also be family, or people, or justice, or peace. It almost doesn't matter, as long as it is a source of good.

What *does* matter, as I learned from my experience in Pastor Davis's youth choir—both being a part of it and leaving it— is that faith in something bigger than myself was the true source for finding faith *in myself*. This gave me the confidence and inspiration to question everything around me and think for myself. It formed the foundation and the safety net that I needed to go out into the world, fulfill my purpose, and hopefully do special, amazing things.

Right now is another moment where my skeptical side would say, *Oh yeah, is that all it takes? Wish upon a star and everything will be sunshine and kittens and rainbows?* The answer is *NO, lil' Miss Skeptical Side!* This is just the beginning. Everything you do after this is built on that foundation.

If you're going to try anything new or scary or big, you've got to have faith—you're going to need it for those down moments when all your hard work feels like it's not going anywhere, when opportunities slip through your fingers or change on a dime, when people tell you that you can't do things or that you're not good enough. Faith *in yourself* is going to give you the strength to persevere and the courage to question everything those people say to you. What do they know that you don't? Why are they right and you're wrong? Why should you listen to them? (The answers to those questions are: nothing; they aren't; and you shouldn't.)

Never underestimate the power and importance of faith—it is the sister to hard work. Just as there is no excuse not to do what needs to be done, faith in yourself can actually help you accomplish those tasks. Armed with faith, I think people can do almost anything.

And I know *you* can.

CHAPTER 5

BE YOURSELF, BE OPEN TO THE PATH

Q: If you could travel anywhere, where would
you go?

A: I'd love to go to Australia because I've never been
there and I love koala bears and all those other
crazy-looking animals with weird names. Not the
ones that can kill you just by looking at you; I'm
talking about the nice ones. I'd also love experiencing
the culture of India because I love the saris they wear,
and I love curry.

————————————

Once Tike and I got to Los Angeles, I did stand-up comedy
for three years with no rest and no real progress beyond little
crumbs of stage time that I could piece together.

If you don't know much about the stand-up comedy world, let me try to describe it for you.

The typical comedy club is a small, dimly lit room packed with small, dimly lit tables, and about two hundred to three hundred seats. In most towns, at least these days, there is just one legitimate club. In bigger cities like Los Angeles, San Francisco, Houston, or New York City, there might be three or four clubs. The owners of these clubs are usually guys—though sometimes it's a woman, like Mitzi Shore who founded The Comedy Store—and they make most of their money from parking and alcohol, so there is almost always an expensive valet stand at the front door, and a two-drink minimum at the bar. That means, if you come to a comedy show, on top of paying for parking and for your ticket to get in, you also have to buy two drinks (they don't *have to be* alcoholic, but that's normally how it goes), and be prepared to spend two hours surrounded by drunk people—including, sometimes at least, the person up on stage.

Stand-up comedians are a unique group of people. They're often very smart, but they're also usually outsiders who see the world differently (that part drew me in), and don't like what they see (that part did *not*). They talk about adult topics like drugs and politics and race a lot. They're pretty vulgar sometimes, and very insecure the rest of the time. At some clubs, hanging around the comedians can feel like high school—there is lots of gossip and backstabbing, and it can be exhausting.

That said, I have admired every good comedian I watched perform. Having the courage, night after night, to stand up on a little stage, all by themselves, with only a microphone and a stool and the jokes in their head, and perform for a tipsy crowd ten feet away from them who let them know every minute or so, with their laughter or their silence, just how good or bad they were that night . . . well, that's a tough thing to do. You really have to be able to bear the pressure and commit to the hard work that goes into making stand-up comedy your career if you choose to put yourself through that, day in, day out. And they do.

As a result, there's usually a strong bond between comedians. They bond over stories of bombing onstage the way mothers bond over baby pictures. The really successful ones wear the bad times like badges of honor and hold on to them as reminders both of how hard things used to be, and how far they've come. They talk about the helplessness they feel when nothing they do turns the night around, and the thrill and joy they experience when they finally get that big belly laugh. Listening to them tell their stories—comedians *and* moms, I guess—you get the sense that these people are walking some kind of preordained path that has been laid out in front of them. I won't say it is like a "calling," but it is definitely a blessed opportunity they can't ignore. I knew that feeling firsthand from my time on the stage (and I can't wait to feel it again as a mom!).

What makes the stand-up comedian's path so difficult, on top of all the hard work and potential humiliation, is that they don't get paid much by clubs. When you're starting out, you can make as little as $20 per set. Even the most popular comedians at clubs in big cities will only pull in a few hundred dollars per set unless they're headlining the entire show. That's why most nonheadlining comedians will try to get up onstage at every club in town on a given night to cobble together a decent payday.

It's sort of the same logic behind doing collabs when you're first getting traction on YouTube. When I get together to do a video with Colleen and her husband, JoshuaDTV, for example, we don't just do one video for my channel, we do one for each of their channels as well. That's three videos instead of one, exposing each of us to three different audiences and potentially tripling our views. All in one day. What a YouTuber is trying to do with multiple videos and increased views, a comedian is trying to do with multiple sets and an increased paycheck.

On a regular day, if there are three clubs in a city and each club has two shows, that's six possible sets you can do if the owners will put you on the list and you can drive fast enough to get to each one in time. If you're lucky to make $100 per set, that's $600 for the night. And make no mistake, you're going to *work* at night, and only the night—during the week, clubs will have two shows, one at 8 P.M. and one at 10 P.M. On the weekend, there might be an extra show at midnight.

I know vampires with better hours.

Now, if you feel like you've gotten to know me a little over the years on my YouTube channel, let me ask you a question: How much of what I just described sounds like the GloZell you've gotten to know? If you can't answer that question because you are too busy laughing, *ding ding ding!* You're 100 percent right.

To start, stand-up is late-night, and I love to sleep. Most comics are young white guys (especially back when I was starting out); I'm a proud black woman. Comedy is often very vulgar—it celebrates the vices—whereas I don't smoke, don't drink, and I'm not raunchy. Maybe if there was a Muppets comedy club circuit I might have found my groove, but if there is ever a puppet at a comedy club, the guy pulling the strings is usually making it say and do very, very bad things. Comedians as people can also be overly possessive and unhappy—I've always wanted to just have fun and share that fun with as many people as possible.

Originally, I did stand-up because that was my path to getting discovered, but over time I was also doing it as an escape from my troubles after my divorce from Tike at the end of 2003. I could live without a man who put his mother ahead of our marriage, but without our pets, the apartment became a very lonely place. The best way to avoid the loneliness of an empty apartment is to not spend time *in* an empty apartment, and the one place I knew I could go where there were people was the comedy club. I never had to worry about being home alone at night because I was always at work.

In the middle of the summer of 2006, something began to gnaw at me: stand-up comedy no longer felt like the route I was supposed to take.

When I first dreamed of coming to Hollywood, it seemed successful stand-ups had it made. Jerry Seinfeld. Roseanne Barr. Rosie O'Donnell. Bernie Mac. Ellen DeGeneres. Ray Romano. Each had a major TV show, something I very much wanted. But slowly, that changed. All those comics whose shows I loved were long gone from the airwaves. *Ellen* was over. *Seinfeld* was over. *The Rosie O'Donnell Show* was over.

The Bernie Mac Show was over. *Everybody Loves Raymond* was over. An entire era was over. Suddenly, reality shows were becoming the big thing, and the few sitcoms that were still being developed by the networks were going to improv comics and really talented writers who could act—not stand-ups. I'd done a little improv with The Groundlings, but not a ton, and I wasn't a writer. The goalposts had moved on me—and it wouldn't be the last time that happened. As I started to reevaluate how I could make it in entertainment, I also started to rethink the world of stand-up comedy entirely, and my place in it.

I was a comedian, but I wasn't a *stand-up* comedian. Carol Burnett was a comedian and *she* didn't do stand-up. She sang and danced and did sketches to get her own show—so there *was* another way to do this.

Hardest of all for me over those three years on the stand-up comedy scene was that in order to get more stage time and better spots in a show, the club owners had to believe I could get people to come see me. It was simple comedy club math: People × Drinks = Money. The more people I brought, the more drinks they ordered, the more money club owners made.

But since burying myself in work after the divorce, I hadn't really gotten to know anyone outside my church (the fact that I even went to church already set me apart from a lot of other people in the industry). And asking the humble members of the First Christian Church of North Hollywood Disciples of Christ out in the Valley to come see me at these places over the hill in Hollywood close to midnight, where my "coworkers" would make graphic jokes about sex, drugs, violence, and religion, well, that was just uncomfortable for everyone.

It says something about the wonderful people from my church that many of them did come out to my shows and I am forever grateful to them for their support. I owe those ladies my sanity, I owe them gas money, and I owe one of them in particular for the next phase of my career.

Her name is Tina. Tina is one of those beautiful people who open their heart and their home to you when you don't even know you need it. Tina invited me to a barbecue at her house for July Fourth that year. It was a perfect summer day: temperature in the mid-80s, sunny, blue skies, no humidity, just a light breeze. It was the kind of day that makes people visiting L.A. never want to leave. Kids were playing in the pool, the grown-ups were chatting, and we were all eating delicious food. I was tired because I'd performed the night before and had only gotten up a few hours earlier, but there was something about the day that got me talking and confiding in Tina about my struggles with my direction in life. This was big for me, because I struggle with opening up to people.

"I always thought I would do stand-up comedy, then I'd get discovered by *The Tonight Show,* and then eventually have my own show," I said. "But now I'm not sure that's the right thing for me to do."

"You're not sure? How will you know?" Tina said.

"I don't know," I said. "I've prayed about it, and I've worked very hard and paid my dues, but I don't seem to be getting anywhere."

"Maybe you need some different inspiration."

"I suppose so. I don't know." I was truly lost.

"I don't know if you knew, but I work at NBC," Tina said. "I can put you on the list to go watch a taping of *The Tonight Show,* if you want. You can go as often as you like—maybe you'll be inspired there."

I've never heard an angel sing, but if I had to guess, it probably sounds a little like the words that just flew effortlessly out of Tina's mouth. She threw the offer out there so casually, on any other day it might have just floated right over my head, but on this warm holiday afternoon, it sank right into my heart. It felt like Tina had thrown me a lifeline when I needed it most.

By the way, this is why, when you're trying to figure out who you are or what you want to do when you grow up, you should join every group that will have you and go to every party you're invited to. And when you get there, treat everyone with respect and love. It's the Golden Rule of show business, or any business for that matter: Treat everyone like they are important and could introduce you to just the right individual or idea or institution (like *The Tonight Show*).

In 2006, *The Tonight Show* was still being hosted by Jay Leno. Jay was a clean comic like me, and he made millions of people laugh like I wanted to, every single night.

Tina was onto something. I'd always been a Leno fan, ever since he started at *The Tonight Show* by guest hosting for Johnny Carson in the late '80s and early '90s. Maybe he could be a role model to learn from as I tried to break into the business.

With that in mind, the next week I went to my first taping. The show filmed in Burbank, just down the road from where I lived in Studio City, so it was easy to get there. The whole day was the coolest, most Hollywoody thing I'd ever done. I was on the VIP list; I got to go backstage. If there had been a special reserved parking space for me, I might have moved into it.

Looking back, there was no single reason for what was about to happen, but I decided to *literally* take Tina up on her offer to go as often as I liked. I went back the next day, and the day after that, and then a fourth time the day after that. I spent the whole week there in Burbank, fascinated by the entire experience. Even standing in line hearing what people were talking about was fascinating because they came from all over the world. I paid attention to what they laughed at (and didn't), and I would try to use those observations to my advantage in my stand-up.

I went to *The Tonight Show every day for the next two years*. Neither Tina nor I could have possibly known at the time what might become of her kind gesture, but it would end up being a turning point in my career. Between 2006 and 2008, I went to *six hundred* shows. I was a fixture at the studio, behind the scenes, and on the street. On a typical day I'd get there before 10 A.M. and leave after the show taped, about 5 P.M.

Malcolm Gladwell says you're supposed to practice something for ten thousand hours to become a master. Well, I stacked up at least half of that being at *The Tonight Show*. If you count up the time I was also putting in onstage, I was getting pretty close to the mythical 10K. But for *what?*

About a month in, with the encouragement of one of the pages (a page is like an intern for the TV network who gives tours and ushers the audience at tapings—think Kenneth on *30 Rock*), I started writing a blog called *glozelllovesjayleno .blogspot.com,* where I interviewed people in line for the show since I knew Jay never got a chance to meet anybody in line.

At the time, I didn't even know what a blog was, or why you'd have one. And as I'd find out later on, the pages didn't really know why I should have one either. They were just trying to suss out who I was, and what I was writing in my notebook. Nobody had any idea what I was doing there or why I was at the show every day, so they were probably a little paranoid. Maybe they thought I was Jay's secret spy, like a mystery shopper.

On the blog, I also taught my readers the ins and outs of coming to see a taping of *The Tonight Show:* how to get seats in the front row, how to get tickets if you didn't have them already, what usually happens on Mondays versus Thursdays, how to get food and not lose your place in line, how to get a picture with Jay, everything. Nobody was doing that, and I figured if it made the experience better, it would make the show better, and everyone would be happy. Eventually, it got to a point where the blog developed a large, loyal following, and people would come to see me as much as they were coming to see *The Tonight Show*. We built a community in the comments section of the blog. They were the first GloZellots, or GloBugs, or GloWorms. (We hadn't figured out a name yet.)

As all this was happening, something else was changing too, first slowly then all at once: I stopped doing stand-up comedy regularly. In the beginning, it was because I felt like I didn't have the time, but that wasn't true. I had the time, I just didn't have the desire. Now I had a more fun outlet for my creativity. And I didn't have to beg for stage time to get it.

Tina's opportunity hadn't been a lifeline after all—or, at least, it wasn't *just* a lifeline—it was the beginning of an entirely new path. At first this new path ran alongside the stand-up comedy path, so I could do both. But it wouldn't be long before the *Tonight Show* path started to diverge and go off in a different direction. I could try to keep straddling the paths, but the further they diverged, the harder it would be for this girl to keep her footing. I had to have faith and make a jump. It was something, at the time, that I did instinctively, without a net. But since then, it's an idea I've heard a lot about from, of all people, the comedian and *Family Feud* host Steve Harvey.

What a lot of people don't know about Steve Harvey is
that after every episode of *Family Feud,* he likes to talk to
the audience for a few minutes. He is a stand-up comic by
training, and a great one, so doing crowd work like that
comes naturally to him. After one show, he got to talking
to the audience about life, and recognizing your gift, and
needing to jump with it if you ever want to truly live. What he
didn't know was that the cameras were still rolling, and soon
the video made it online and went viral. It is so inspiring—I
must have watched it a dozen times; you should check it out.

"God when he created all of us, He gave every last one of us a
gift at birth," Steve started. "He never created a soul without
endowing them with a gift. You just have to quit looking at
gifts as running, jumping, singing, dancing. It's more than
that. If you know how to network, if you can connect dots, if
you draw, if you teach, some of y'all fry chicken better than
anybody else. Bake pie. Some of you cut hair, color hair.
Some people do grass."

Those gifts Steve was describing weren't just talents, they
were all the different paths someone could take. Then he told
a story:

"I got a partner who never wanted to go out with us because
we stayed out too late. 'C'mon come out with us, man.' And
he'd say 'Nah, I've gotta get up early tomorrow and cut Miss

Johnson's grass.' We kept laughing at this dude. 'Cutting grass? How much they pay you for that?' Today, he's got a landscaping company in Cleveland worth $4 million. All he did was cut grass, but he was gifted at it. You have *got* to identify your gift."

What Steve said next puts it all together:

"Standing on the cliff of life, when you see people soaring by, doing remarkable things, have you ever thought that maybe those people haven't just identified their gift, but they are also living in that gift? The only way for you to soar like them is to take that gift that is packed away on your back like a parachute, jump off that cliff, and pull the ripcord."

I'd done exactly what Steve was talking about—I'd identified my gift, a long time ago in fact. I could make people laugh, I could entertain people.

So why had I come to feel so stuck and unsuccessful?

Being an entertainer is really just a job title—it's what I put down on my taxes. Making people laugh is how I do that job, and jokes are just the tools of the trade. If I really look inside at my true self, the honest truth is that my gift is the ability to make people happy.

Unfortunately, I'd lost sight of this true self in the years leading up to the fork in the path I was now straddling.

Since marrying Tike in 2000 I had tried to change myself so his family and friends would like me. He told me it wouldn't work, that they would never like me, but I still tried. I made myself small and quiet and invisible (hard to imagine, right?). I didn't want to draw attention to myself because it would draw attention away from him, and I knew whatever attention I received would be judgmental and negative. Even my relatives got in on the act—they liked having someone in the family married to a *doctor*. They'd say, "Don't make waves, GloZell. Be grateful for what you have."

When we split up, you'd think that the true me would burst out like a jack-in-the-box with a curly weave. But that's not how it works. If you squish something down long enough, sometimes it stays squished, and you have to work hard to stretch it back into its normal shape.

After the divorce was finalized, I started to see glimpses of my true self onstage and, later on, in line outside *The Tonight Show* with people I helped or interviewed or met from the blog, but I still hadn't fully reconnected with my true self or recognized my real gift. I certainly never let it rip.

When I did finally let it rip—when I jumped like Steve Harvey begged his *Family Feud* audience to—guess what happened:

I found YouTube. It was yet another path opening in front of me, even if I didn't know it right away.

———————————

Today YouTube is my home, not Florida or California. If my true self had a passport, it would list YouTube as my official "Place of Birth" on the first page. But in late 2006, two months after I started my *Tonight Show* blog, YouTube was just another company Google had bought for a billion dollars. And it was another two years after that before I even started posting videos on my site.

At first the process was straightforward, if not a little slow. I would create a video from the day, then post it directly to Blogspot and *voilà*, I was done. But then Blogspot started moving really slow. I don't know if it was more people starting blogs, or more people doing video, or both, but upload times slowed to a crawl. The experience was like watching a video of a sloth eating vegetables, or a sloth crossing the street, or just about *any* sloth video. My best friend, Jacqui, suggested I upload my videos to this site called YouTube, and then copy and paste the links directly into blog posts as a workaround.

So that's what I did.

It was so easy—I started making multiple videos each day and throwing them up on YouTube. I didn't think about it as my *channel;* I just copied the links to the videos I thought would be good for the blog and pasted them over there.

You have to remember, I'm talking about early 2008. YouTube was still relatively new and much different than it is today. It wasn't a "platform" then—heck, I don't know if that word even existed, except to refer to the thing you stand on when you're waiting for a train (or the thing I stood on, waiting to slide down a fireman's pole).

Before long I started getting pretty good at making videos, though. I learned how to do an intro, how to conduct an interview while holding the camera, how to sign off. And then over about a month's time—between April and May of 2008—I did three videos that outperformed my average daily video by like 1,000 percent. One even did more than a million views. Not that I knew this—I never paid attention to how many views I got (which is another pro tip: the more you care about some random thing like traffic or impressing people, the less fun you'll have, and the work will suffer).

I didn't even have a cell phone or a camera—I had to borrow a computer just to post stuff (I'd use the one at my church from time to time as well). The only "hot spot" I'd ever seen was the big yellow one in the sky that burned Patrice when we were kids and all the white people standing in line for *The Tonight Show* who forgot to bring hats. The idea that I could track my video views, or that I *should?* C'mon now.

It took my bff, Jacqui, to call me up one night to tell me about the video that had gone over a million views. She was good lookin' out on stuff like that for me. I didn't believe her at first—was she sure they weren't like spam views, or a typo? A million views? For one of my videos? *Why?* I didn't know why then, but I know why now: I'd jumped onto this new path with both feet.

With faith in myself and my work ethic, I found the courage to let more of my true self come through.

It wasn't more than a few weeks later that I was pulled out of the line outside *The Tonight Show* by a page and escorted into the green room. Contrary to what you might think, the green room was not designed especially for me; it's where guests of the show wait before coming onstage. There's a nice sofa, some comfy chairs, lots of yummy snacks and drinks on a table. I thought, *This is it! They must have seen my Nad's video and want me to do a sketch. Or be a guest! OMG OMG OMG!*

I could not have been more wrong if I guessed they wanted me to guest host while Jay was on vacation, like he used to for Johnny Carson. They sat me down, and some security officer I'd never met before announced that I could no longer attend tapings of *The Tonight Show* and that I was hereby barred from entering the premises.

Ehhhhh-xcuse me?!?

I couldn't even comprehend what they were saying. *The Tonight Show* was everything to me. It was all I had. It's not like they were paying me—I wasn't employed by the show, yet I was basically being fired. It was like a scene right out of that *Seinfeld* episode when Kramer gets fired from a job he doesn't have.

I couldn't believe my ears. Why don't you just turn Disneyland into a cemetery while you're at it, because California is clearly trying to kill me! With my world circling the toilet and my stomach in my shoes, my first thought was, *What are they going to do without me?* But that was really just my brain covering up the real question in my heart, "What am *I* going to do without them?"

I didn't know why they kicked me off the lot. The rumor was that it came from Jay Leno himself, but I'll never know.

Jay Leno had not just been a role model for me in comedy and entertainment, he had also been a mentor (from afar) in life as well. He had an incredible work ethic; he almost never missed a day. He didn't go on crazy long vacations—in fact, his dedication reminded me a lot of my dad. On weekends Jay still did stand-up at The Comedy & Magic Club in Hermosa Beach, or he'd fly over to Las Vegas and do shows there. He didn't need the money, he just loved what he did, and I loved him for it. (You know it's true too, because it says so in the name of my blog, *glozelllovesjayleno*.)

A lot of people have someone like that in their lives: a mentor; an idol; a hero. Maybe they dream of meeting that person one day, but rarely do they think, *One day that person is going to fire me and ban me from their presence.* (A friend of mine was once fired by a boss they'd known their entire life . . . their mom. Getting kicked out by Jay felt even worse.)

When I heard that Jay might have been the one who banned me from *The Tonight Show*, I was crushed. I realize now I probably came off as an annoying pain in people's sides to some extent. Was I just an overly enthusiastic fan or an obsessed crazy person? I was totally harmless, but how could they know that? Still, I wasn't really all that surprised when I got the news. I was used to being judged unfairly by people my whole life, often for things that were out of my control or not even my fault.

When I think of that day being booted from *The Tonight Show* lot, I compare it to six months earlier when I'd gone to a taping of *The Ellen DeGeneres Show*. Ellen's show filmed on the same studio lot as *The Tonight Show*. It was her first year doing her Christmas giveaway, so we all got gifts—I got a watch and a log that smells like coffee when you burn it in the fireplace. But the best gift was when Ellen came over during the show to talk to us. I'd managed to end up in one of the front rows, so I was right in her line of sight—the tall young black woman straight losing her mind. When she asked my name, I got so excited that it cracked her up and she talked about me on the show the very next day! I remember thinking at the time, *Yeah, THAT'S how you do it Jay! That's how you treat your most loyal fans!* I don't know why I stayed so completely dedicated to Jay Leno and *The Tonight Show* after that; I'm just glad something good came out of it.

———————

Looking back, I'm so thankful that my time at *The Tonight Show* ended when it did, because I might still be there otherwise. It's a very real possibility that scares me when I think about it because in those moments in 2008 my path was forking again. *The Tonight Show* was going one way, and YouTube was taking me another.

Plus my self-worth had become so wrapped up in that show that it wasn't healthy. Now, with nothing else occupying my time—no husband, no stand-up comedy, no *Tonight Show*—I immediately started working more on my videos and quickly had my first truly viral smash hit: "My Push-Up Bra Will Help Me Get My Man."

That video was total improv. I was actually headed to the park to film something else when I came across a car fire on the road and flipped open the camera on a whim. It happened during the day on a Monday, and if I'd still been at *The Tonight Show*, it never would have happened. And just like the car I passed on the street, the video exploded. (Years later, it's still in my top five most popular videos ever.)

———————

Not long after, I got recognized in public for the first time. It was at a Costco, by a young girl who followed me from aisle to aisle as I helped myself to the free samples that make Costco on Saturdays the happiest place on earth if you're still kind of poor (Kirkland cheddar cubes are delicious, #sorrynotsorry).

In those days, I went to Costco every Saturday, so at first I thought maybe the girl went shopping with her mom every Saturday too, and that's why she was staring at me—because *she recognized me as that lady who loved the samples*. It turns out that she had actually seen the Push-Up Bra video and watched it, like, fifty times.

I started getting recognized more often after that, and a funny thing began to happen: people would ask about my "GloZell character." Character? Isn't this how people act when they're with their friends or just being themselves? The question confused me. My "on-camera personality" (I'm still not even comfortable saying those words) isn't a character. It's not contrived at all. It's me. In many ways, it's actually me at my most comfortable and most authentic. Anybody who knows me—going all the way back to Calvary Presbyterian School—isn't surprised by the person they see in my videos. They know that this is my truest self. They understand when I talk to them about what I do that this is the path I have always belonged on.

I've learned since my early YouTube days, and from getting to know other YouTubers and trading stories with them (like comics or moms do), that the question about "my character" is pretty common. "Normal people" struggle to understand people who have big personalities. We aren't putting on airs, I promise—it's just the way we are when we let our true selves come out and play. It's something anyone can do, at any age.

And it's not just running, jumping, singing, and dancing, like Steve Harvey said. It's anything—from his partner with the landscaping business in Cleveland, to my mom in Orlando who calls me fifty times a day and makes crazy hats out of stuff, to you and whatever gift God endowed you with and packed in your parachute: if you can figure out that gift, accept your truest self for who it is, and remain open to every path you encounter, then you don't ever have to be afraid to let it rip!

CHAPTER 6

HATERS GONNA HATE

Q: What's your favorite Thanksgiving food?

A: Stuffing. Some people call it dressing. It's whatever your grandma makes with all that love and about a hundred thousand calories in it and makes you want to go to sleep five minutes later.

———————

Haters gonna hate. It's a reality I tried to deny for a long time, but ultimately, I had to accept.

Have you ever noticed how haters only come after the things you really love, particularly when those things are going well? It's like they have a nose for not only our weakest points, but also for what we value the most. If you don't care about fashion, nobody bothers to say anything about your clothes, if they even notice at all. If you would *die* for fashion—and you spend a lot of time and energy developing your personal style, picking the *exact right outfit* every day—that's when the haterade turns from a trickle to a tidal wave.

I used to think haters were just angry or jealous people (sure sometimes they are), and if I only had a chance to talk to them and let them get to know me, their haterade would dry up. But as I looked a little closer at the things haters say and do, and I learned a little about a few of the haters circling my life, what I found wasn't anger or jealousy at all—what I found was fear.

The people being mean to you? They are *afraid* to do what you had the courage to do, which is be true to yourself, and be open to the path in front of you. They are afraid of being different, afraid to take a step in a new direction, because they're worried they'll hear the same kind of nasty judgment thrown at them that they throw at you. And instead of taking responsibility for their own fear, they hate on you for taking control of yours. It's like you're a reflection of all their fears and failures, and instead of looking into the mirror, they want to smash it to pieces.

And here's the hardest part about dealing with haters: they can come from any corner of your life. They can be younger than you, or older, or the same age. They can be boys or girls. They can be friends, neighbors, family members, or perfect strangers.

I'll give you an example: Remember my friend Abby who switched schools at the end of fourth grade? She was my best friend in the entire world. I know that sounds silly to say as an adult, but when you think about it, she was my friend from the time I was five years old until I was nine years old. That means when she left, we'd been friends more than half my life!

You want to know why she left Calvary Presbyterian? It wasn't because they bought a new house outside the school district (this was a private school), or because her dad got a job somewhere else and they had to move. No, it was much worse than that: her parents removed her at the end of the school year because our fourth-grade teacher—it's hard to even write this, but her name was Mrs. Stuckey—convinced them that their daughter was spending too much time with just one girl and it was becoming a problem. Yes, she meant *the black girl*. Mrs. Stuckey was worried about Abby, and how such a tight bond between us might affect her future relationships with other kids.

This doesn't happen with race as much anymore, but with kids who are LGBTQ, or "the smelly kid," or just plain weird, you bet it still goes on. Mrs. Stuckey initially registered her concern by making phone calls to Abby's parents, and amazingly, to *my* parents. Then there were letters, and parent-teacher conferences. Then more "official" kinds of letters. I was still four years away from graduating, but my friendship with Abby had already graduated from "different" to "a problem." Mrs. Stuckey wasn't worried about me or how our bond might affect *my* future relationships—oh no, of course not. Don't be silly.

I didn't know any of this was happening at the time, mind you. My parents loved me very much and protected me from the drama. They couldn't protect me the following September though, when the roster for the fifth-grade class arrived in the mail, and Abby's name wasn't on it. (Getting banned from *The Tonight Show* was nothing compared to how I felt when I found out about Abby.)

How does a teacher do that to a young child? Or to two young children? Today, most people would immediately say, *How awful and backward she was! What a horrible racist!* Oh, she was definitely racist—I don't care if she doesn't consider herself racist, actions speak louder than words—but as an adult, when I really think about what happened, painting Mrs. Stuckey as an ignorant racist is just too simple.

No, Mrs. Stuckey was a hater of a different type: she saw these two young girls with no hate in their hearts; two girls who didn't see color; two girls who shared an amazing bond at such an early age, and she was jealous because she'd never had anything like that in her life. And the fact that she was jealous made her angry. *How can these nine-year-olds have something I've never had but always wanted?*

The thing is, I bet Mrs. Stuckey could have had a friendship like ours. Why couldn't she? Anyone can have a friendship like that. It's a matter of opening your heart. She was a good teacher; actually, I remember liking her. I would have been her friend; she was perfectly nice. Maybe she was always afraid of what other people thought, and that's what held her back, or maybe she was scared of being her true self, so she tried to keep other people in their categories just as she kept herself in her own lane. She thought it was better to shatter the mirror instead of look into it, I guess. How do I know all this? I don't, it's just a guess, but I watched a lot of *Oprah* and *Dr. Phil* so I'm pretty confident. Plus, don't we all know someone who is bound by these invisible ropes and chains?

And you know what else? I bet she never once, not for a second, stopped to think about me crying in my room about it. Empathy—taking the time to think about someone else's feelings—can overcome all sorts of hatred. It's a superpower we all have. Not enough people use it.

The next time you are considering doing something that might affect another person in a bad way, just stop and try a little empathy. You'll be amazed at how it feels.

_____

In the aftermath of Abby's disappearance, my parents were there for me as I tried to make new friends and make the best out of the last four years at Calvary Presbyterian, but that was about the extent of my support system for a while.

To be honest, I wasn't getting much love from my extended family, especially on my dad's side. This time, I don't have a teacher like Mrs. Stuckey, or a talk-show host like Jay Leno to point to as the culprit—no, this time it was MaDear's doing, and she didn't even realize it.

After my grandfather died, MaDear kept an open door at her house. Kids and grandkids could come and go as they pleased. The small table in the kitchen would always be set, and there would be food on the stove, and drinks in the refrigerator. She was doing that thing a lot of people do who struggled as parents the first time around: she was trying to be a better grandparent. My dad valued her effort, and since he'd become "successful"—financially speaking—he was able give her a little bit of money every time we came over to visit.

MaDear was a proper southern black woman, so she was always grateful and appreciative. Never one for subtlety, she showed that gratitude in a very direct and obvious way: by giving my sister, DeOnzell, and me preferential treatment over the other kids. If we were in the living room watching TV—even *The Price Is Right*, which was her favorite because she was in love with Bob Barker—and we wanted something to drink or we just wanted her attention, she would give it to us. That might not sound noteworthy, unless I tell you about the time one of our cousins tried the same thing, with far different results.

That day, we were all watching *The Price Is Right*, and my poor cousin asked MaDear for a glass of water. Nowadays, you'd just go in the kitchen and get it yourself, but back in the day—and especially at your grandparents' house— things were more formal, and you never took yourself into a different room other than the bathroom without permission.

"Wait for the commercial break," MaDear said.

"But, MaDear, I'm really thirsty," my cousin said.

Bad idea.

There was a pause, and then MaDear got up from her chair. Looking right at my cousin, she grabbed a stick that was holding the living room window open—it was a hot, hot day—

and right there and then set about giving that boy a solid beating. (I bet the day Bob Barker retired from *The Price Is Right* was the happiest day of my cousin's life. I can't even imagine what he does at a restaurant when he wants a refill of his water.)

It was hard enough to witness, but my sister and I also knew that it would never have happened to DeOnzell or me, which in some ways made it worse. And it didn't stop there. Whenever we'd come over to visit, she'd let us eat at the little kitchen table, but she'd make all the other grandkids eat on the floor. It didn't matter if some of our cousins were already at the table when we came in, she'd move them to the floor. She didn't think we were *better* than them—she loved us all equally—she just had an old-school way of showing appreciation for my dad's financial generosity.

I can't imagine what it must have felt like to be in my cousins' place. And what made those moments even stranger for me is that I *always* wanted to eat on the floor! That's where our cousins were hanging out eating, and coloring and playing games. That's where all the fun was at, but MaDear wasn't having it.

Guess who didn't like this situation that much either: the rest of my dad's family, that's who. And guess who they took it out on? Yes, you guessed it: DeOnzell and me. (Not that I blame them, I'd be upset too.)

My aunts and uncles already had a rocky relationship with my dad, and now it felt like they were passing down their frustration like an heirloom to their kids, and there was nothing anyone could do about it.

What I learned from this tough situation was this: it doesn't matter what your orientation is, what your skin color is, whether you grew up rich, poor, with two parents or five parents—nobody should ever be punished for something they were born into. They didn't have a dang choice in the matter. And it's scary to feel like you don't have control of anything, like your fate is sealed. Who wants to believe they're unlucky by birth, while someone they are related to and grew up with seems like they can do no wrong?

The point is, you never know when or where or why your haters are going to pop up. And because of that, you can't spend your whole life trying to anticipate, run away from, or defend against them. You just have to live your life, be as true to yourself as possible, and trust your path. If my husband and I are blessed enough to have more than one baby, and they grow up to have kids of their own, I will make sure that I take to heart that lesson and all the others I learned from

MaDear—the great ones, and even the not-so-great ones that led to all this family strife.

I don't mean this to sound like I had some horrible childhood, or that I was a victim of all these vicious haters while I was nothing but pure love. I loved my school, my teachers, my friends and classmates, my church, my family. But I've been a hater too; I think we all have at one time or another. It's part of growing up and figuring yourself out, no matter how old you are.

After my divorce in 2003, for instance, I hated on pretty much all guys for a while. I was afraid I'd never meet another good man I could marry and have babies with, and I blamed *men* for that. I hated on *them,* instead of focusing on myself, and doing what needed to be done to overcome that fear of rejection and loneliness. Do you think I had some hate for my ex and his family too? You bet. But that was the hurt talking. It did nothing productive for me.

The flip side of growing up and figuring yourself out is learning that there are some things in this life you cannot change. One of those things is how people feel about you. People will judge you for aspects of your character that are either not your fault, not in your control, or the worst of all: you'll get judged for those critical parts of your personality that you couldn't change even if you tried. That's not an easy thing to deal with. The best way I have found for dealing with those times is to do something Mrs. Stuckey should have done all those years ago: look in the mirror. I think about the times I've been a hater or been hated on, and I ask myself: *What aspects of the other person's character was I afraid of? What aspects of my character were* they *afraid of? Do any of those things need to change? Can* they *change?*

I'm a passionate person—it's who I am. I am the daughter of Ozell Green. I was a black girl in a mostly white private school in the American South in the 1970s—and no, I had no say in the matter. Given all that, is it any wonder I have trouble trusting new people and tolerating fake people? Yes, I can be skeptical sometimes. Can those things about me change? Sure! Should they?

I don't know.

All these things are part of what defines me as a person, but they don't define me completely, even if that is all people want to see when they judge me. There is nothing I can do about that. *Haters gonna hate.* You can let it get you down and eat you up, or you can do what Princess Elsa of Arendelle says and let it go, *LET IT GOOOO!*

I choose to let it go. It's what helped me get over *The Tonight Show* thing and onto making more YouTube videos so quickly. It's how I avoid drowning on all the haterade that can get poured into the comments sections of my channel and those of my friends. And in early 2015, it was how I didn't let myself get affected when Rob Lowe slammed me on Twitter after I interviewed President Obama. He posted a picture of me from the Cereal Challenge and then wrote:

"Hold up. Is it true that a woman who eats cereal out of a bathtub gets to meet with the President and the Prime Minister of Isreal does not?"

I've been around the block enough times to know Rob Lowe's issue wasn't with me. I'm sure he wasn't questioning my career path, or my life choices. Maybe he was afraid of how media is affecting politics, or how the Internet is influencing our culture, or maybe his toilet seat wasn't warm enough when he woke up that morning in his giant Malibu house as (still) one of the most beautiful men in show business. I don't know, I've never met the man. His tweet stung for a hot minute, I'm not going to lie, but once I let it go I was able to see the bright side—*at least my haters are beautiful*—and then turn the other cheek.

After that, I teased him about his spelling (*Isreal?* Really, Rob?), but I didn't poke fun at his men's skin care line, like a lot of mean-spirited people do on Twitter. He's passionate about it, so he should be proud of it. It can be scary to try

something new like that when everyone expects something
else from you.

Maybe one day I'll get to meet him and we will laugh about
this together, and then he'll remember me when there's a role
available in his next Hallmark Lifetime movie for a sassy,
self-assured black woman who takes Jesus's message to heart
and turns the other cheek when confronted with prejudice
by an incredibly handsome white man who isn't very good
at spelling.

That's how you have to look at things if you want to be
happy and do cool stuff in this life. You can't let yourself get
distracted by negativity, no matter where it comes from.

In school it can be students *or* teachers. At home it can be
family or neighbors. Online it can be commenters, and trolls.
In life, it can be anyone . . . even Rob Lowe. You just have to
remember that it almost always has nothing to do with you.
It's always about them.

Do you want to be the person who, at ninety years old, is, like,
"I wish I'd kept playing the trombone" and regrets quitting
it because someone else said it was "gay" or "dorky"? Do
you want to be the person who maybe ends up married to

the wrong partner because you let an overbearing parent or friend bully you into dumping someone who might have been "The One"? Imagine where Jay Leno would be if he'd listened to his haters—people who'd booed him offstage, or agents who said he wasn't funny enough, or people on Twitter who called him names when he wanted to come back to *The Tonight Show*. Good Lord, imagine where a woman like Carol Burnett would be if she let all the sexist haters in the 1960s prevent her from breaking new ground for women in comedy! Imagine where *I'd* be if I cared about all the knocks . . .

I believe in positivity and looking forward. I don't want to think about what could have been, actually—I want us all to think about what could be. The only thing standing in the way of that is a little hard work, a little faith, and maybe a couple haters. But forget about the haters.

Haters gonna hate, it's what they do. Don't worry about them—you just do you.

CHAPTER 7

FIND YOUR ABBY

Q: Who is your celebrity crush and why?

A: It was One Direction because they are all so
beautiful, but now I don't know anymore. Dang it,
Zayn, why'd you have to go and do your solo
thing? Now One Direction is *None* Direction!
Sad face emoji.

Since discovering YouTube in 2008 I have been blessed to find
myself among a large, supportive group of happy, creative
silly people whom I get to call my friends.

There's Colleen Ballinger-Evans, and her husband, Josh Evans
(a.k.a. JoshuaDTV); Jenna Marbles; Joey Graceffa; iJustine;

Kingsley; and Heart Defensor. We come from all over the country, we're different ages and races and orientations, but we also share a deep desire to have fun, make entertainment, and connect with people. We're like coworkers, all part of this big crazy company and our bosses are . . . *you guys*, the fans. Many of us were fans of each other's before we were friends, so really our friendships are a giant mutual admiration society.

I can't speak for them, but for me, our relationships only began to develop when I learned to accept my truest self, and let myself walk the paths that had opened in front of me. Once I did so, it was like all these people I would have otherwise never met were just waiting there, eager to join up with other people walking their own paths.

It isn't always that way, though. Sometimes the path is lonely for stretches, especially at the beginning. You ever post a video and have it get zero views? Ever sit there and watch the comments *not* roll in? That's lonely. It'll make you doubt everything. Other times, the path itself isn't lonely, you just manage to wander off it for a while and get lost. I have a few friends who are okay with that—they like being by themselves, out exploring, doing other things. They look forward to their quiet alone time. If that sounds like you, well then, you're in luck, because it means you don't need to go searching for companionship and you don't need to grab hold of every person you meet along the way and go skipping down the path arm in arm like Dorothy and her friends in *The Wizard of Oz*. It's okay if you'd rather be like Dora and Diego, bouncing around the world having adventures like wonder twins. Or you can fly solo for as long as you're happy. It doesn't matter.

Still, whether you're a loner, or the life of the party, or somewhere in between, you need to find that one person who understands you better than anyone else, maybe even better than you know yourself. This person can be a boy or a girl, a friend or a family member, a teacher or an employer—in fact, they can come from anywhere (like a hater). They can even change over time as you get older, go away to school, move, or get a new job. The only thing that matters is that this person appreciates you for who you really are, because this is going to be the person you rely on when those lonely stretches get too lonely. Their voice is going to be the one you follow when you've wandered too far off the path and you are trying to find your way back.

———————————

The first person who helped me back to the path I should have been on was Abby, which shouldn't surprise you considering how much I've talked about her (and the fact that her name is the title of this chapter).

Abby didn't do all this for me intentionally—unless she is a secret crazy baby supergenius, that is! No, she just accepted me for *who I was*.

On the first day of kindergarten, when all the little white-walkers were scaring me, Abby came over and said, "Hi, do you want to play blocks with me?" And with that we went over into the corner, where all the toys were stored, and played until class started. I latched onto Abby like a koala bear and didn't let go for five years.

From kindergarten through fourth grade, we did everything together. We ate lunch together, played blocks together, sat next to each other, colored together. I never missed a day of school in my life (*perfect* attendance), but if Abby was ever absent, I would just sit there by myself, in my chair, waiting for school to be over or Abby to walk through the door—whichever came first.

Except for little things like "getting taller," and "learning how to read and write," Abby never changed as we grew up together. We could be goofy, play piano and sing songs, or just play by ourselves for hours. When you're young, and

different for reasons out of your control, it can be hard
sometimes to explain why you might feel unsettled. You're
not smart enough or aware enough to work out what's going
on. In retrospect, finding a friend like Abby gave me my first
experiences *embracing* what made me unique, instead of
trying to cover it up, and in the process it actually made me
feel normal, and calm. I think it's why I loved school—I got to
see Abby, so I got to be me.

When Abby's parents took her out of school at the end of
fourth grade, I struggled to find new friends, and I struggled
to trust people generally, which made making friends even
harder. I worried that if I went full-koala, I might wake up
one day and my new friend would be gone, just like Abby was.
I wasn't sure if I was ever going to have a connection like that
with someone ever again.

If the last four years at Calvary Presbyterian weren't going
to feel like one giant long spelling test, I had to find my
next Abby. I didn't know that consciously at the time—I just
wanted another best friend. For a couple years it felt like it
would be Patrice. We spent a lot of time together at school,
and as the first person to ever come over to my house for a
sleepover, that alone gave her a special place in my heart. You
remember Patrice, right? The girl my mom accidentally tried
to boil and peel like a Gulf shrimp before turning her into a
sandwich. Yeah, that didn't go so well.

My struggles didn't end with a sunburned friend
unfortunately.

The loneliest times for me were during high school and
college. Sure, I had friends in both places—I just never had
that one person I could really put my trust in.

In high school, my parents kept me in the Calvary
Presbyterian system, but Calvary Presbyterian High School
was *even smaller* than the grade school. Not only did I
have fewer potential friends to choose from, but they were
the same ones I already knew and had already not fully
connected with.

You would think after nine years as one of the only black
students at a small private school, my parents might have
given me a chance to spread my wings and meet more people
in a larger, more diverse environment, say, the public high
school in our neighborhood? Nope. My mom and dad were
very concerned that if I attended the public school, I'd be
around kids from the neighborhood who were less well off
than me—they were kids who knew I was Ozell Green's
daughter, and they might hate on me for it. They were
worried I'd hear things like:

"Oh you Dr. Green's daughter—you think you got something?"

"You think you special because your daddy got a store?"

"Lil private school girl gotta go to the big school now, huh?"

Their fears for me were palpable: "GloZell, those public school kids from the neighborhood would have eaten you alive," my dad told me once when I asked him why they chose Calvary for us.

(Thanks for the ringing endorsement, Pops!)

"You were soft, baby," my mom agreed.

"We knew Calvary wouldn't be easy, but we knew you wouldn't have to deal with as many of those mean girls either," my dad said.

"And if you did well," my mom said, "and made something of yourself out of that private school—well, we knew that you'd earned it, and would be fine the rest of the way."

They were right—both of them—of course. They were *parents*.

I started at community college in Orlando to be near my dad, and then, as I've said, I basically became a commuter student to the University of Florida after his second amputation and he could no longer work at the pharmacy day to day.

College was only two hours away, so every Friday Dad would pick me up from school, and then the following Monday he would drive me back. I'd love to be able to tell you how he made the drive—having no legs and all—but I'm still not sure how he did it. All I can teach you is how to ride in a car being driven by a man with no legs: HANG ON TIGHT.

Was this arrangement ideal for making friends or making it home in one piece without having a heart attack? No, but like I've said: no excuses. You have to do what has to be done, even if it means riding in the family van with a man who can't feel the pedals with his prosthetic legs, and who once got his shoe stuck under the accelerator in rush-hour traffic.

People talk about all the crazy times they had living away at college, but very few of them can top some of the experiences I've survived—like driving home on the highway at full speed, then hearing a rattle followed by a loud thump, and then turning around to see your dad's wheelchair fly out the back of your van straight into traffic.

When I think back to that day, it reminds me a lot of the moments immediately after I broke my ankle at the Streamys. There is this brief period of eerie silence when you stare at each other in stunned disbelief, followed by total scrambling chaos. Drivers behind us laid on their horns and swerved, trying not to hit the wheelchair, and then each other. Dad stopped when he finally realized what was happening . . . but he stopped in the very middle of the freeway.

"What are we going to do, Dad?" I said.

He looked at me.

"Go get it."

And I'm, like, "You go get it!"

"I have no legs!" he said. Sure he wasn't "lying," technically, but it was all very convenient for a guy with his prosthetic leg currently holding down the brake pedal.

So I opened the door, prayed to God (which was common while riding with my dad) and stepped out onto the freeway, crying hysterically. It's not like he pulled off to the side of the road when this happened. The man stopped literally in the middle of the freeway. One false step from me as I hopped out and I would be swept away like a duck in a river.

It took a couple minutes, but I finally reached the wheelchair. I quickly picked it up (it had fallen on its side), rolled it over to the van, tossed it in the back as fast as I could, and hopped in the front seat. And do you know what he said?

"You better not have scratched it." He turned away from me for a couple infuriating seconds and let his comment sink in. When he turned back, he saw the look on my face, and couldn't hold it together any longer. He cracked up, and we both cried with laughter.

I never had a chance to talk to my dad about that crazy incident—actually, I was never able to talk to him about a bunch of that medical stuff—but I think he knew all his issues had an ongoing impact on my college experience. I think that's why he made jokes about his situation—to make it not seem so bad, and to give us something to bond over. I think he wanted it to be our "thing."

When he got his prosthetics, for instance, the doctors tried to give him a set where the plastic matched his skin tone. But my dad being my dad, he took the white ones instead and said, "At least now my bottom half will get treated better than my top half!"

Dad's favorite joke was to take me with him whenever he had to go shoe shopping. Bad shoes had gotten him into this mess, and he was not about to let shoes be a problem with his prosthetics, so we would get new shoes anytime the soles on the old ones would get too worn down. If he ever got a salesperson who didn't know who he was, he would try to scare them by unfastening his prosthetic so that when they lifted his leg to try the shoe on, the whole thing would come off in their hands. You'll never see someone question their career choice faster than a person who woke up one morning not knowing that their day would involve holding another man's leg in their hands.

But there were also days when he didn't feel like getting out of the car, so he'd just send me in to get a new pair of shoes.

"But I don't know what size you are," I'd protest.

"Here, use this," Dad would say, as he pulled off one of his prosthetic legs.

That wasn't all. Dad would deliberately park as far away as possible, while still being able to see the front door of the shoe store, so he could watch me take his leg inside. He watched every second of the performance—down the block, at the stoplight, across the street, then into the store and up to the counter—like it was theater. You could have stolen the groceries right out of the backseat and I don't think he would have noticed. I can still hear him laughing.

If you're wondering where I got the courage to get up onstage at a comedy club, or persevere through getting booed at

Showtime at the Apollo, or eat a bunch of hot sauce and wasabi, or jump down a fireman's pole and snap my leg in half, or make fun of myself, or share with the world my fertility challenges . . . you can find it at the bottom of an old black man's fake white leg.

———————

Now that I think about it, my parents were my first Abby, before Abby was my Abby.

Were they my Abby the whole time, even when I thought I didn't have an Abby? I don't know, but I will always be thankful for the blessed support of my parents. They mean the world to me.

Yet here's the thing—your parents can never really be that one special person, no matter how hard they try, or how much you want them to be. They know your spirit better than anyone—of course they do—but they only really know the person that *they* created and raised. They don't know the version of you that you have created for yourself.

Think about it like this: In school did you ever get into a fight with a mean girl who wouldn't stop picking on you? The fight gets broken up, you get hauled into the principal's office, they call everyone's parents, and then the mean girl's mom says something like, "My Janay is a sweet innocent girl. I raised her to know right from wrong; I don't believe for a second she would ever do something like that!" Janay's mom isn't lying; she believes everything she's saying. The Janay *she* knows— the one *she raised*—is a sweet innocent little thing who was taught right from wrong.

The problem is, that Janay doesn't exist anymore. She's dead. R.I.P. Li'l Janay!

Instead, Janay is now a fourteen-year-old psychological terrorist who makes her friends call her "Juicy," who cusses at teachers, and then picks on girls smaller or shyer than her to feel better about herself, all because she has trouble reading and developed before all the other girls.

Her mother doesn't know this version of Janay. To her, "Juicy" is a total stranger, because she was created by Janay out of her sight. But I bet you there is someone who *does* know Juicy really well, and it's probably her best friend. Now, Juicy's best friend should smack some sense into Juicy and help guide her back to the path she has clearly strayed from . . . but that's another story.

The point is, as great as your parents are, the older you get, the less well they know the person you are trying to become. They will try their hardest to get to know that person, but it will never really happen. And it will never be as easy—for you or for them—as it will be for the person (or people) you have *chosen* to let in while you figure out who your true self is and what you want your life to be. It's *that person* you need to find.

For almost twenty years now, the person who knows my true self has been my best friend, Jacqui.

Jacqui showed up in my life after college, in 1999 or 2000, while I was still in Florida. At first, I didn't like Jacqui at all. I was cast in a play called *Carousel,* in Orlando, and one day at rehearsal this stunningly beautiful white girl with long wavy hair and perfect skin walked in like she was floating on a cloud of dreams. The best way I can describe her before I got to know her is that she was the kind of girl you don't let your boyfriend talk to.

Jacqui introduced herself to the cast and crew, then very demurely started telling us what to do. *Oh, heck no!* Wannabe Miss Florida 1999 might be polite and get all the attention and the best parts, but she doesn't get to boss us around too! Well, technically she did get to, because she *was* the boss, or the co-boss—turns out she was one of the codirectors of the play.

Jacqui and I got along fine, though, in the beginning. She wasn't an instant-Abby, but we got to be friends as a group of us from *Carousel* started hanging out. We all wanted to be actresses or entertainers of some kind or another.

The ringleader of our group was a woman named Becca. (Remember the cute blond girl from *Pitch Perfect* who was the leader of the Bellas? She was kind of like that, but without all the nervous barfing.) Becca decided we all needed to be SAG members before we made the move to California, so when we weren't performing together, we bonded and schemed around trying to get our SAG cards.

SAG—the Screen Actors Guild—is the labor organization that represents working actors in film and television. When you join, it's called "getting your SAG card." You can't just sign up, though—you have to work on certain kinds of commercials, TV shows, or movies and then apply. You don't need a SAG card to be an actor or a performer who gets paid—YouTube taught me that!—but there's a psychological boost to having one. It's something you can show to people to "prove" that you're an honest-to-goodness professional actor. (It's also good for convincing your family that you're "making progress" and not just foolishly chasing a dream.)

What they don't tell you is that the *real* benefit to having a SAG card is the health insurance that comes with it. The card is worth its weight in gold for that alone. When you get walking pneumonia or you break your ankle (as I would find out), it's that insurance card you really want, not your mom.

––––––––––

All of us working on *Carousel* called ourselves "Du-Plex," and our plan for joining SAG involved developing some kind of Saturday morning variety show that we could maybe get on one of the local cable channels or perform live, and then take the show with us to California and pitch it to the big TV networks. In reality, we were just a bunch of people who knew one another and liked to perform. And what Becca didn't know was that I already had my SAG card, so I was more about making friends than getting the mythical clearance to be an actor.

––––––––––

SAG card issues aside, I found myself liking Jacqui a lot.

She was my age, in her late twenties, and she was studying for her theater degree at the University of Central Florida (she already had multiple degrees). She came from a family of doctors, I learned, but also found that she enjoyed performing—not in the way a lot of us did, though. She was an introvert who liked to sit back and take everything in, then find her opening and come in with something low-key but really smart.

Weirdly, her combination of beauty, intelligence, and talent made people dislike Jacqui. Through no fault of her own, women were jealous of her, and men were intimidated by her, and instead of handling their own business, they took it out on her. Beauty and brains were for Jacqui what black and bold were for me: *hater catnip*.

Sometimes, when you meet someone as amazing as Jacqui, it takes either a big, formative event to make your friendship solid or a whole stretch of time when you're joined at the hip. Until one of those things happens, you're really just friend-*ly*. Your real besties are the people you've shared *real*, numerous experiences with.

Over the next couple years, Jacqui and I acted in various plays all over northern Florida—we even got jobs playing characters at Universal Studios Orlando. I was Storm and she was Rogue. We never won Employee of the Month, but we were superfun to work with, and kids loved taking pictures with us. The best part of the job was in the off-season, or on shift breaks, when we'd go on all the rides. I swear we were the most fun Storm and Rogue Universal Studios ever had. If you went to Universal Studios in 2002, looking to take pictures with all the X-Men characters, I'd be willing to bet you had the biggest smiles in your pictures with Storm and Rogue.

In 2003, everyone from the Du-Plex theater group relocated to Los Angeles. Almost immediately we lost touch—all of us, including Jacqui and me. I was busy with stand-up comedy and being married (for a while longer at least), while she was going to cosmetology school. I wasn't worried—Jacqui and I are different in a number of ways, but we shared some essential character traits: We didn't like other people's drama; we didn't trust a lot of people, thanks to things from our past; and we didn't have many close friends. And we were both spiritual.

Then in early 2005, I got a call from Jacqui out of the blue. She told me that Becca, our original ringleader, had moved to New York City, and that she wanted to meet up. We met at a Starbucks in Studio City and I must have talked nonstop for an hour catching her up on everything that was going on in my life. Jacqui barely said a word. I thought to myself: *What is up with this girl? Did I do something wrong?* A week later I got another call from her. She wanted to meet up again. We met at the same Starbucks, and again I did all the talking and she sat there stone quiet.

Jacqui is an introvert—a little meek, maybe even a little scared—but she isn't a mute. Did all the L.A. smog fry her vocal cords? Did she take a vow of silence?

As we left, she finally cracked, and it was something small, but huge.

It was her phone—it wasn't broken, but it sure wasn't working right, and the people at the store wouldn't replace it for her. They were going to make her pay full price for a replacement, which she couldn't afford at the time, and she needed that phone for her work and for callbacks on auditions.

Hearing this, something in me clicked over. I said to myself, *Okay, this is my homegirl from Florida. I can't be letting these people take advantage of her.* I had her take me straight to the phone store. I was a girl possessed, like Straight Outta Orlando, Kevin Hart "psychopath girl" possessed.

"Hey! HEY! Who here in charge?!" I was shouting in the middle of the store, like I was robbing a bank. "Who here told my homegirl you ain't fixin' her phone, tryin'ta get over cuz she's just some pretty little white girl?"

Let's pause and remember that this was a cell-phone store in the Valley in the middle of the day in the middle of the week. The employees were community college kids and senior citizens trying to stay active. They had no idea what was about to hit them, and even less of an idea what to do about it.

"Don't make me come back here rollin' deep with my brothers!" [I don't have "brothers."] "And don't make me go online and be tellin' everybody how racist y'all is!" [I didn't have a computer then, and Jacqui was whiter than a Katy Perry concert.] "You best be fixin' this phone right quick or I'ma come correct wit my crew and make it correct!" [Crew? It was me and Jacqui. "Correct?" There was nothing "correct" about the things coming out of my mouth.]

I thought for sure I would get arrested.

Once I'd finished yelling, the manager came over, took the busted phone out of my hand, and replaced it with a new one right out of the box. We didn't even have to fill out any of the long paperwork that used to come with cell-phone contracts. He just wanted us gone, and his life back to normal.

Girl power!

Jacqui and I had walked into the store like friendly reacquaintances, but we walked out as *friends*. It was like we hadn't skipped a beat from our Florida days. We were Storm and Rogue again, only a little older and with a cell phone that worked.

We even got jobs together again—this time at the same spa.

We were two weird peas in a very different-shaped pod who from that day forward became each other's support system and biggest cheerleader. We understood each other; we knew what the other person needed even if she didn't know it herself. Jacqui helped me get over Tike and back into the dating game, and I helped her meet people. She helped me with my Jay Leno blog, and she taught me about YouTube. I taught her . . . how to meet people.

She needed a lot of help.

I probably needed the help even more than she did.

The years between my divorce in late 2003 and really finding my voice on YouTube with stuff like the challenge videos in early 2012 were the scariest, most exhilarating, and most uncertain times of my whole life. Looking back at them, if I hadn't reconnected with Jacqui in 2005—if we hadn't been there for each other—I don't know if I would have had the courage to share my feelings with Tina, the woman from my church in L.A. who worked at NBC. I don't know if I'd even have had the energy to accept the invitation to her July Fourth barbecue. I don't know if I would have had the strength to recover from being banned from *The Tonight Show* potentially by one of my heroes. I don't know if I would have had the wherewithal to recognize the opportunity that YouTube represented, and then take advantage of it. I honestly believe that my friendship with Jacqui, and our deep, spiritual connection, is a huge reason I've been able to accomplish so much and achieve so many of my dreams.

It's easier to accept and love your true self when someone else has beaten you to it. It's way harder to hear the haters when you have a best friend whispering love in your ear. It's not as scary to walk the path in front of you when your friend can see it too, and she promises to be there to guide you back if you ever get lost.

Since my popularity on YouTube really grew I've done a lot of meet and greets across the country and around the world. In the early days, a few dozen people would show up, maybe as many as one hundred. Then, it got into the multiple hundreds. Then, it got big enough that we needed to hold an official event—GloZell Festival—to accommodate everyone. Every event was mostly young fans who wanted a hug, and a picture, and to tell me their favorite video. They'd come up in groups of friends, and soon enough they were talking excitedly to one another while I just stood there smiling. Each one of those young people is amazing, and I love all of them.

But every once in a while, fans who were by themselves would approach me. They were usually a little shier, and maybe a little more awkward, and their hugs were always a little tighter. They'd tell me their names, and then they'd ask me a question that was always some version of: "How do I get to do what you do? How can I be like you?"

Knowing very little about any one of these lone fans, I could tell they were unique, they were creative, they were driven . . . and they were completely lost. My advice was the same to each of them: you need to find that one person in your life who knows the true you better than anyone else, and who will support you no matter what, as you pursue whatever dream keeps you up at night. You don't need a million fans or friends—you just need to find *that one person.*

This is not a revolutionary idea, I know that. It's not just for young people either. It took me *thirty years* to figure it out! If you want to find your true self, and if you want to find your future, you need to find your Abby. You need to find your Jacqui.

Then, you need to hang on to them like a koala bear for dear life.

CHAPTER 8

YOU'RE #1

Q: What is the best pickup line?

A: [Seductively] Is you OK? Is you? Good . . . 'cause I want to know.

When the doctors amputated my dad's first leg, he stopped working day to day at the pharmacy. When they took the second leg the following year, he had to stop working altogether. That didn't mean he stopped caring about his family, however. In fact, I think he started to care *more*.

For my dad, family filled the hole created by forced retirement. We each became one of his little projects, and we were okay with that. The only time we weren't okay with his impulse to help fix things was when he turned his attention to home improvement projects.

My dad was very proud of the home he'd built for us, and he, in turn, wanted us to be as proud of our home and as comfortable in it as he was. So whenever something broke or wore down, my dad turned immediately into Mr. Fix-It. Remember that time I watched him climb up a ladder with shoes on his knees? He was fixing a broken shelf. As he put it, it was an easy patch job, so why bother strapping on the prosthetics? He'd be up and down in no time.

Every time he pulled out that dang ladder we held our breath. We weren't afraid he might fall off it changing a lightbulb or tumble off the roof fixing a leak—no, our concern was based on the fact that brainy science guys who are good at chemistry are usually horrible at being handy. Remember *The Smurfs?* Remember that one hilarious episode when Brainy Smurf and Handy Smurf got together to solve a big problem for Papa Smurf? Of course you don't—because you've never watched *The Smurfs* and have no idea what I'm talking about. My point is, nothing like that ever happened on the show because brainy and handy almost never go together, and my dad was living proof of that. Where the house was concerned, he literally made everything he touched worse.

If he tried to freshen up the paint job on the windows, he'd accidentally paint them shut. If he tried to unclog the big U-tube under the sink, he'd forget to put a bucket underneath to catch all the water that came pouring out after he separated the two pieces of pipe. Hanging pictures on the wall wasn't a chore, it was an adventure! And forget about anything related to electricity—the fact that our house was never responsible for knocking out the power to the entire block, or that my dad never electrocuted himself (seriously), may be the greatest testament to God's grace.

———————

My dad spent practically every waking moment of his retirement worried about, and caring for, his family and friends. He even dipped into his savings to help people. I don't know this for certain, but I think he helped every single person in our family except for one. Do you want to guess who that one person was? That's right—he never worried about himself. *Stress. Anxiety. Tension. Exhaustion.* Those weren't words that you'd ever use to describe his mood. Dad was old school—he just did what needed to be done and made no excuses. Mentally, emotionally, and spiritually he could handle the load. Physically . . . well, that was a different story.

The circulation issues that resulted in my dad's double amputation didn't stop at his knees. They affected his heart, too. Not its capacity to love—he had the fullest heart of anyone I've ever known—but its health and longevity. The restricted circulation put extra strain on his heart. The wear and tear took years off his life.

Imagine trying to drive a car with the parking brake on. You can do it, but you have to push the engine extrahard. Do it for too long and the brakes will wear out, then the motor. The amputations were like taking the parking brakes off to help him ease up on the effort his heart (the motor) had to put in to keep his body (the car) going at normal speed. There was only one problem: he never took his foot off the gas. He did the opposite, actually. He put the pedal to the metal.

Eventually, my dad's heart started to give out. He was tired a lot and then had bouts with shortness of breath. Still, he pushed through it, doing his thing as the head of the family, until the doctors had to go in and do major bypass surgery. This was his third big procedure in less than ten years. (I rotate my mattress less often than that!) Strong guy that he was, he survived the surgery. When they were done, the doctors came out into the waiting room to tell all of us the news.

"He did great," the surgeon said. "He'll live another ten to fifteen years at least." Everyone was relieved. There were hugs and kisses and tears.

Less than an hour later, he was gone.

My family was beside themselves, falling out all over the floor in the waiting room, wailing into each other's chests asking each other, asking God, asking no one in particular, "Why? Why?! WHY!??" The doctors were speechless, too. There were no complications during the hours-long surgery; his vital signs had been stable the whole time. They had no idea why he died.

But I did. I knew why he died: my dad had worked himself to death. His heart had just run out of gas.

Knowing the kind of man my father was, I'm sure he had no regrets about the way he lived his life. He accomplished many firsts for his family name. He built a successful business and a good reputation in the community. He did a lot of great things for a lot of different people. His life had been a full one. But it was still shorter than it should have been, and the reason is because he never put himself first. Everyone and everything came before his own needs. It's why everyone loved him, and why he was gone too soon.

Had my dad put himself first at any point in his adult life, even for a little bit, I'm certain he would have lived several more years. If he made his health and comfort as much of a priority as he made DeOnzell's or mine, I won't say he'd still be here (it's been a long time), but he might have gotten to see some of the biggest moments of my life as an entertainer and a YouTuber.

By the way, I don't know how old any of you are reading this book, but let me tell you something: As a kid, you have all sorts of big ambitions for yourself. You want to be an entertainer, or write a book, or make it to the Olympics. At the same time, most of us don't always have the greatest relationships with our parents. When we're young, we're frustrated with them and feel like they're always up in our business. Then something happens: you eventually get up there on that podium or accomplish that thing you've been dreaming about, and more than anything you want your parents to be there—proud of you. It'll break your heart if they're not there. So appreciate them now, while they're still here.

Did I understand that at the time? Of course not. How many pieces of advice did your parents or teachers give you when you were young that didn't make sense until you were older? Like a *million?* (If you're still young, *wooo child, just wait!*)

When my dad died, I was in my late twenties, married to Tike, doing plays, dreaming of making it out to California. I wasn't thinking about *how* to live a long, full, happy life; I was just hoping it *might* happen.

It wasn't until several years later when I was in Los Angeles, doing *The Tonight Show* thing, that the notion of putting yourself first, of being the number one person in your own life, started to make some sense to me. The first time was on a plane. I forget where I was flying to—probably back to Florida for a holiday or a birthday—but I remember I was actually paying attention to the preflight safety demonstration for once. Most people, myself included, usually tune those things out, all that stuff about the seat belt buckle and flotation devices:

> To fasten your seat belt, insert the flat metal end into the buckle. To release, lift up on the top of the buckle. Seat belts must be worn low and tight across your lap. Whenever the "fasten seat belt" sign is blah blah blah . . . <headphones> . . . zzzzzzz.

But that particular day, when the flight attendant got to the oxygen mask part, one sentence in particular sent a little shiver down my spine:

If you are traveling with a small child, or someone else that requires assistance, put your mask on first, and then assist the other person.

She was saying that you need to take care of yourself first, then you can go take care of everybody else. The physical reason for that instruction is because at high altitude, it only takes three or four seconds to lose consciousness if the cabin loses pressure. You're no use to the people who need your help the most if you're unconscious!

But my dad would totally have been the guy to put his mask on second . . . or third . . . or not at all. He'd have been running down the aisles making sure everyone in our family was set, then every other woman and child and then maybe, *maybe* if there was time, he'd think of himself. In his short life, he put the mask on every one of his family members multiple times before he ever thought of putting his own on.

There's a very famous saying that I have thought a lot about in my own life since my dad passed. It goes: "God helps those who help themselves." Have you heard it? I bet you have, probably from your parents when you asked them for help with something and they tried to make you figure it out for yourself because they were busy doing something else.

You: "Dad, can you please get the cereal down for me?"

Dad: "God helps those who help themselves, sweetheart."

You: "But Dad, it's on the very top shelf, and I'm seven."

What it means is that you can't expect other people to fix your problems if you don't at least try to fix them yourself first. This applies to every kind of problem: friend problems, love life problems, math problems, money problems. The solving part should always start with you.

This is hard for a lot of people, but not because they are lazy, or they want to make excuses, or they're selfish. No, I think it's hard because too many people aren't selfish *enough*. They don't put themselves first, and as a result, when things get bad in their lives, they have no idea what to do because it feels like it's happening to somebody else. Or worse, they get blindsided by the problems because they never saw them coming. How could you, really, when you're not focused on your own priorities?

I experienced this very thing back in 2011 after Tike had left, when *The Tonight Show* was done with, and I was building my YouTube channel. At the time, Jacqui and I had been reconnected for a while, and our friendship was going strong. We were besties—she was my sister from another mister. But eventually, I found myself doing something with her that my dad had done with us in his final years: I made Jacqui one of my projects.

Here was this intelligent, talented, drop-dead gorgeous woman who was introverted and shy, but a firecracker when she was onstage. She was spiritually driven, but never judgmental. She was never mean, but maybe too nice for her own good. And most confusing of all for me, she was perpetually single. She'd have dates with guys who seemed promising, but they'd never go anywhere, or the guys would turn out to be phonies. I struggled to understand not just how she did not have a man, but how did she not have *the* man. How had some confident, successful Disney-prince-looking guy not swept her off her feet? This was Hollywood for crying out loud—they invented this kind of fairy-tale stuff. If it was going to happen anywhere, it was going to be here. When it didn't happen enough times in a row, I finally took it upon myself to find Jacqui a man. I was gonna marry this girl off!

For months, maybe even a year or two, if I wasn't making a video or doing a meet and greet or going on a talk show, I was trying to draw Jacqui out of her shell and hook my girl up. Heck, sometimes even during those things while I was working on my career I was also working on finding Jacqui her Mr. Right. I'd bring her with me to parties and events, introduce her to my YouTube friends, make her sit next to a guy if we were at a big dinner. I'd tell anyone and everyone who would listen how amazing my friend Jacqui was. That doesn't work very well with introverts, I realize, but I couldn't let her stay in her head 24/7/365. If she had it her way, she'd just stand in the corner observing and analyzing everyone— not in a mean, judgmental way, but in the way curious intellectual types do.

One year I invited Jacqui to GloZell Festival and she spent the entire time off to the side of the stage, just watching, not talking to anyone. When I caught up with her at the end of the event, and thanked her for coming, I asked her if everything was okay. She said she had *the greatest time!* Go figure. I was even more determined to find her a man, whether she liked it or not!

Eventually, Lord only knows how, Jacqui met someone. He was a doctor, which was perfect, not because she was sick but because her family were all doctors so they would speak the same language. He was also older. Not like Morgan Freeman older, more like Denzel older, so she wouldn't have to deal with the insecurity of younger men. And most important, he adored her. Of all the men she'd dated while I'd known her in L.A., none of them *adored* Jacqui as much as they *drooled* over her, like she was an In 'n' Out burger.

I was a little suspicious of the doctor at first. He hadn't done anything wrong; I think it was actually the disappointment talking from not being the one who found him for her. Their relationship moved very quickly—they were in love before you knew it, which was fine by me. Their problem wasn't the speed with which they fell in love, it was the time it took for either of them to *do* anything about it.

Being her naturally shy, introverted self, Jacqui wasn't about to take the lead and talk about moving in together or getting married. And her boyfriend, being older, wasn't just going to jump in blind with both feet. As you get older, those big decisions are harder to make because there are only so many left, and there is less time to do something about them if you're wrong. I understood where they were both coming from—I recognized that getting engaged was an important decision at an important time in both their lives. That said, I wasn't trying to hear any of that nonsense. Boy better put a ring on that! (Beyoncé would have been so proud.)

When it finally happened, I was happy for them and relieved. Then I saw the ring. Future Mr. Jacqui had picked it out himself. It was just a band, and of course I thought she deserved a diamond that sparkled as much as she did. Jacqui loved it because she loved him, but I couldn't allow her to live her new life with a plain ring. That might mean a plain wedding, which could mean a plain marriage. Then where would she be? Jacqui was anything but plain.

I had to do something. So, in the summer of 2011, I wrote them both an e-mail and put him on blast, in the hopes that a little reverse psychology would get Jacqui the ring, the wedding, and the marriage I thought she deserved.

The subject line was *"This ain't gonna happen!"*

The e-mail was short and sweet:

"Girl, he ain't gonna marry you. He's never gonna do it, so you better get out now. And that ring is pitiful too.   xo GloZell"

That was not one of my finer moments, I admit. We all do things in our lives that seem to make sense at the time, but later on with some distance, we regret because we missed the bigger picture (they were in love!). This was one of those instances. The thing was, at the time, I felt like I had to do it. As a proud black woman with a big personality and some experience with being let down, I felt like it was my job as the best friend to say the things that Jacqui would never say.

Jacqui had already seen the power of that personality for herself at the cell-phone store when we first reconnected. This time was no different, except for the bridge I had just burned. Jacqui ultimately got the ring and the wedding I felt she deserved . . . not that I was there to see either, since right after I sent that superharsh e-mail I ghosted.

I completely disappeared from Jacqui's life.

I quit Jacqui's life for a very good reason: before you get up in other people's business, you should take care of your own. And I hadn't done that.

As things were starting to come together for Jacqui, they were going nowhere for me. I'd spent so much time focused on building her up as my project that I neglected to give my own life that same kind of attention and care. Charity starts at home, right? Well, Jacqui was on her way to having a comfortable home, a nice car, a man who loved and adored her—and I had given myself very little shot at any of those things, and for the first time I admitted to myself that I wanted those things, too.

Don't get me wrong, my life wasn't in some kind of downward spiral. My videos were going well enough, and my YouTube channel was growing at a decent rate. I was doing what I'd always wanted to do: entertain people and make them happy.

I'd also met a guy back in Florida whom I liked a lot. The problem was that everything had kind of stagnated, which was a very weird experience for me. Since coming to California in 2003 I would reach these forks in the road every couple years, pick one and take that path, then experience these majorly exciting changes. Stand-up comedy, then *The Tonight Show*, then YouTube. I was constantly growing. Now it felt a little like I was standing still, or at the very least running in place.

I realized I had done with Jacqui exactly what my dad had done with our family. I put her oxygen mask on first before I even thought about putting on mine, and as a result I kind of went unconscious in my own life. If I was going to solve this problem, I needed to put myself first. No one else could do it for me—not my fans, not Jacqui, and not God (especially if I didn't try to help myself). By getting her happily married off and then burning the bridge behind me with that e-mail, I knew Jacqui would be taken care of, and I'd have no choice but to take care of myself. Once I did that—once I really made myself the number one person in my life—it wasn't long before I went from running in place to running like a chicken with my head cut off (in a good way, trust me).

A couple months after my relationship with Jacqui ended, I did my first challenge video—the Cinnamon Challenge.

The video opened a new path on my YouTube journey that has led to many life-altering opportunities. On the back of it, I crossed one million subscribers and then two million subscribers . . . *in the same year!* To date it is still my most popular video with forty-seven million views and counting. How nuts is that?

Around that same time, I also met Colleen Ballinger. We were in Utah filming an episode of a web series together, and we clicked right away. Even though Colleen was much younger than I was, we had a lot in common as performers. We were both singers and actresses, we'd both done a number of plays, we both had a goofball sense of humor, and we both loved making people happy through our work.

Back in L.A., Colleen and I started meeting every week to talk about our videos and our goals. Eventually, that led to a number of really successful collabs, our Sir Mix-a-Lot duet at the Streamys, and a new lifelong friendship.

Needless to say, it's been an amazing few years. And what's crazy is that while none of this would have been possible without Jacqui's friendship and understanding of the true me, it also would not have been possible if I had continued to rely on her. I ghosted her, not because she was holding me back—I would never say that, especially since it isn't true— but because I was holding *myself* back.

I was not putting myself first or prioritizing my own happiness. I put off dealing with problems and fears in my own life, by focusing on those of my friend. What's funny is that when you do that with someone you don't know very well, people call it being judgmental and critical. But when you do it with someone you are incredibly close to, they call it kindness and selflessness.

I believe the real issue is that both things—being too critical or being too kind—prevent you from growing as a person and fulfilling your dreams. Being true to yourself and open to the paths that make themselves known to you are a big piece of the puzzle, but if you wait for someone else to tell you which path to follow, then the puzzle immediately changes its shape. The path you take is no longer really *your* path. Those dreams are no longer really *your* dreams.

And it all stems from losing your focus on yourself.

I know there are a lot of people out there who probably disagree with me—especially adults. Some of them will tell you to ignore this advice completely. All I can do is talk to you from the perspective of my own experience, as someone who has been an outsider in nearly everything I have tried to accomplish. To grow, to lead a long, happy life, and to achieve big, new things in this modern world, you have to make yourself the most important person in your life. You have to be your own number one fan. You have to put your oxygen mask on first.

That means studying for final exams instead of Facebook creeping on your ex's new bae. That means fixing your own flaws instead of gossiping about other people's. That means working on your talent instead of judging everyone else's. That means figuring out what makes you happy instead of worrying about pleasing your parents or your teachers or your partners (they won't want to hear that one).

I'm not going to sit here and tell you it's easy, but I also won't lie and deny that it's absolutely necessary. Jacqui understood that probably better than I did at the time, which is why once the pressure equalized in the jet plane that my career had become and I reached a comfortable cruising altitude, I was able to finally take off my oxygen mask and we were able to reconnect . . . again.

CHAPTER 9

LEARN FROM YOUR MISTAKES

Q: What was it like to interview President Obama?

A: Completely amazing! I would say it's a dream come true, but never in my dreams did I think I would have an opportunity like that. The funny thing was that I made, like, every mistake possible that day.

I walked around the entire White House barefoot because the fancy shoes to my nice grown-up outfit hurt my feet (I wanted to wear a tutu and Crocs, but that wasn't "respectful" enough).

When Obama arrived in *Marine One* (that's the name of his helicopter) and walked in from the garden, I lost my mind and started screaming. The people from Google and YouTube who set up the event were worried I wouldn't be able to handle myself during the interview. The people who worked at the White House loved it though, because they see it every day and it's boring to them now. Hey, the brother takes a helicopter to work and lands it on his lawn. That's cool whether you're the president or not.

Before the interview, the security and protocol people instructed us on how everything would work. President Obama would come over, we'd stand up, extend our right hand, he'd shake it, then we'd sit down for our interview. At no time were we to touch the president after that or hand him anything (not for security's sake, but because stuff carries germs and getting the president sick isn't usually a good idea). So what did I do? I went straight in for a hug and I handed him three tubes of glittery green lipstick for the ladies in his life.

I was a little flustered with the lipstick, because I remembered right then that we weren't supposed to hand him things. I tried to take it back, and in the moment I got all turned around and called the First Lady his first wife (the blogs loved that one!).

I'm not going to apologize for going in for the hug, though. The man is fine. He smelled so good too. Like sandalwood, and power. And, hey, thanks to Rob Lowe, I found a larger grown-up audience and got millions of more views. A win-win all the way around!

Anyone who has met me IRL or watched my videos knows that I have no problem meeting or connecting with people. I can keep it real with anyone, which is probably why my life has become a giant collection of funny, nutty, "I can't believe you just said that," out-there people. I mean, there are all my YouTube friends, who kind of speak for themselves. And then there's my mom and Jacqui who no one would ever accuse of being average or boring.

That said, the most calm, levelheaded, "normal" person in my life today is my husband, SK. And I had to kiss a lot of funky frogs to meet that prince.

The string of guys I dated after my divorce from Tike were so weird I wouldn't believe it if I hadn't lived it. Each one was a bigger mistake than the one before him. Had I known then what I know now, I might have been able to avoid these bumps in the road. Then again, if I had, I might not be where

I am right now. But in life, you don't just take the good
with the bad, in most cases you only get the good by getting
through the bad.

The first guy I dated was Dwayne. I met him at a club, and
I never go to clubs. In all my years in L.A., that was still the
only time I'd ever gone to a club. There's nothing wrong with
clubs if you love to dance—which I do—but I also like to
interact with people and have conversations, and clubs are
not good for that unless you enjoy conversations that go like
this:

Him: Hi.

You: **WHAT?!**

Him: I said "hi." What's your name?

You: **I CAN'T UNDERSTAND A THING YOU'RE SAYING!**

Him: You know you're fine, right?

You: **NO, I'M NOT IN LINE. THE BATHROOM'S OVER
THERE.**

Dwayne was nice looking, he wore a suit, he didn't mind
dancing a little, and he was taller than me, which is
important since I'm six feet tall with my weave on. I liked
him. After a couple songs, we managed to find a quiet corner

at the club and we got to talking. He was sweet and confident and respectful, so we hit it off. We asked each other all the normal getting-to-know-you questions. Our answers were all totally normal. Then I asked him what he did for a living.

"I'm an architect," Dwayne said.

Wow, I thought, *how could I be so fortunate?* I wasn't being superficial, I promise. I wasn't thinking about how much money he made. I was just excited that I had met someone who didn't have a Hollywood job—not a comedian, or an actor, or a producer. He had a real, normal job, and it was one that meant he could build us our dream home with a deck that a hot tub fits into, and a gazebo in the backyard where we could have romantic dinners in the summer.

You know, if we got that far.

"What kind of stuff do you design?" I said.

"You know when you go through the drive-through at a McDonald's or a Burger King, how you order at the menu, then drive around to the first window to pay and then the second window to pick up? I designed that whole system, with the windows and the overhanging roof to protect your food from getting wet."

I didn't know what to say at first. I guess *somebody* had to come up with the design for a drive-through system. It's pretty incredible when you think about it—a lot of people have benefited from that model. There are tens of thousands of them all over the country, maybe even hundreds of thousands if you include banks and coffee places. Heck, even pharmacies have drive-throughs now.

"That's amazing," I said. "So where do you live? I'm over in Studio City."

"I live over the hill too," Dwayne said, "with my mom."

That sound you're hearing in your head right now is me slamming on the brakes.

Oh, heck no! I already had one momster-in-law ruin my relationship; I had no interest in going back for seconds. Tike had been a mama's boy, but at least he had had his own place to live. I think Dwayne could see the doubt on my face.

"It's my house though. My mom lives with me, not the other way around. She's a quadriplegic, so I take care of her." *Awwwww.* (See, that's what happens when I let my skeptical side dominate my hopeful side.)

Dwayne and I exchanged numbers and we started talking regularly over the next few weeks. He traveled a lot for work, and you know how insanely busy I am, so we didn't get to see each other all that often. Our relationship developed primarily on the phone.

One night we were talking, filling each other in on how our week had gone, and he kept saying how tired he was. *Gosh, I'm tired. I'm so exhausted, I can barely keep my eyes open.*

"Why are you so tired, Dwayne?" It felt like he was begging me to ask him.

"I drove a lot of miles last night," Dwayne said.

"Why were you driving around so much?" I asked.

"Because I'm a truck driver," he said, like it was nothing. Like I hadn't been imagining him as one of the twins from *Property Brothers.*

"What do you mean you're a truck driver? When I met you, you said you were an architect."

"Well, I do both," was his response, "because truck driving is just something fun to do and I like doing that."

"So you're an architect . . . and a truck driver? You're a truck-driving architect." I'm sure I sounded a little suspicious, but I gave him the benefit of the doubt. I mean, how could I *not?* He was tall, a good dresser, he's got *two jobs* now, plus he owns a home that he lets his quadriplegic mother live in so he can take care of her. That's a catch in my book!

A couple weeks later we were on the phone again, and this time it wasn't fatigue that got in the way of our conversation, it was his mother.

"Dwayne! Dwayne!" I could hear in the background as I'm telling him about my day.

"Hold on," Dwayne says.

"Dwayne, you want this dinner? I brought you some dinner."

I'm, like, *brought you some dinner?*

"Okay, Mom, thank you," he says.

So she leaves, but then I hear these footsteps going down a flight of stairs. *Clump, clump, clump, clump.* Now I'm confused. Maybe that wasn't his mom. Maybe it was his sister, or his mom's nurse, or maybe she brought it upstairs in one of those stair elevators. Before I can ask, he tells me to hold on again.

"You forgot the hot sauce!" Dwayne shouts. Fifteen seconds later the same person is back with the hot sauce.

"Dwayne, who is that you're talking to?" I had to ask finally.

"That's my mom. I told you I live with my mom," he says, again like it's nothing.

"Oh, I remember," I said. "She *brought you dinner?*"

"Yeah, she's a good cook." Either this boy is dense, or I am missing something here.

"I thought you said she was a quadriplegic."

"Oh yeah, yeah, yeah," he stammered, "not all the time though. It comes and goes."

It comes and goes. *It comes and goes!?* I'm no doctor, but I'm pretty sure that's not how being a quadriplegic works. As someone who has experience dealing with a parent who endured major disability, I can assure you that being a quadriplegic limits your ability to *stand* in front of a hot stove, let alone *walk* up and down stairs to deliver hot sauce to a triflin' little mama's boy.

CAN YOU BELIEVE THAT?!?

Dwayne is trying to play me with some sob story and he doesn't even have the intelligence or the decency to learn about the lie he was trying to tell? Needless to say, that was the end of Dwayne the Drive-Through-Designing Truck Driver with the part-time quadriplegic mother who sometimes forgets his hot sauce. I wouldn't have cared what he did for a living, and I wouldn't have cared all that much that he lived with his mom, but I can't date a dummy *and* a liar.

You don't get three strikes in the court of GloZell.

The next guy I dated was superfamous, but I'm going to call him Tommy because it's never good to kiss and tell in Hollywood.

Tommy was only *regular* famous from TV back when I met him, but he's gotten *super*famous since he started doing movies. I met him at a comedy club where I was still doing some shows, and he dropped in to see what was going on. After I got offstage that night, he sent one of his boys over to get my number, because that's what guys do when they're famous in L.A.

What was I going to say? Tommy is supertalented, he's funny, and he has already made it in a field I'm trying to break into. Of course I gave his boy my number—at the very least Tommy might have some advice for me.

We kicked it for a few weeks. I saw his house (no fake quadriplegic mom). It was fun. But then I had to break it off.

It was nothing Tommy did. He was sweet and very confident. He took care of his family (they *actually* lived with him, and not the other way around, like Dwayne). Tommy had swagger and pull—he even got food delivered from the International House of Pancakes any hour of the day, which of all the things about him was the coolest, because IHOP doesn't deliver. Tommy can get it any time he wants? Oh my goodness!

My friends were furious with me when I ghosted. They were, like, *He could hook you up with an agent, get you acting roles, take you on vacation to places where the beach has that sand that's as soft as baby powder!*

I'll be straight—that sand thing was the real toughie when we went our separate ways.

If I had been younger, and fresh off the freeway from Florida, maybe I would have listened to my friends and let Tommy take care of me for a long time. That's what a lot of girls do when they get to Hollywood—they find a guy like Tommy, and they hang on for dear life. Not like a koala bear either, more like a parasite. That wasn't me, though—that *isn't* me.

There's this thing with famous people where they become the center of their own universe and the world kind of revolves around them. Sometimes it's because they've gotten really good at making themselves number one in their own lives, but they've wandered from their path and lost hold of their Abby. Other times, it's not that they're conceited or selfish, it's just that they have so much talent and charisma that they cast a really long shadow.

That last one was Tommy. I wasn't mad at him for it, but I'd just spent three years in Tike's shadow, and doing that again in a different relationship wasn't something I was interested in. I was trying to find my own voice and do my thing in entertainment, so I realized pretty quickly that it was never going to work. I was a grown woman and I didn't *need* Tommy to survive.

———————

About a year later, I was at a barbecue place near my church called Uncle Andre's when I met two guys standing in line behind me. One of them was a little shorter and very cute, the other was taller, not as cute, but well put together. The taller one had a degree and he was getting his doctorate, so he did all the talking. His name was Jamal. The shorter, cuter guy was his brother. His name was Shaqkobe.

I'm not joking. Shaqkobe. Like Shaquille O'Neal and Kobe Bryant, the famous basketball players who were still teammates on the Los Angeles Lakers when I first arrived in L.A. Obviously I didn't believe him—that name was probably some hustle they ran on girls (they probably learned it from an architect-trucker named Dwayne out on the open road).

I could tell Shaqkobe was used to my kind of skepticism, so he pulled out his wallet and showed me his driver's license. Sure enough, there it was: Shaqkobe. Sometimes, I think if I could have only one wish, it would be to take my iPhone back in time to 2006 so I could have snapped a picture of his driver's license as proof.

Still, Shaqkobe was *cute,* so I wrote my phone number down on a napkin and went on with my day. I didn't hear from him for weeks. Then one day I bumped into him at Ralph's, the big grocery store chain in Southern California, and he looked a mess. His hair was grown out and needed a trim. His clothes were a little ratty. I gave him the benefit of the doubt because who really goes to the grocery store looking like a million bucks? We talked and he apologized for not calling.

"We should go out," Shaqkobe said.

"Yeah, okay. You still got my number?" I said.

"Nah, I must have lost it," Shaqkobe said, "gimme it again."

I guess I could understand how he lost it; after all, I *did* write it down on a napkin right as he'd ordered his lunch— maybe he used it to wipe sauce off his chin. So I gave him my number again, and this time he called. We agreed to go out to a movie that weekend.

That night, Shaqkobe showed up at my house right on time and I met him out front. (Good rule of thumb to my young people out there: when you're older, and you live in an apartment, never let someone you don't trust yet know exactly which front door is yours. It'll save you a lot of grief, trust me.) I walked outside and he was waiting to open the car door for me, which was very nice, but there was something off about this car. I couldn't tell if it was a rusted-out hoopty, or if it was just dirty, or if it was just the orangey streetlights making it look bad. It was too dark to be sure, so I didn't want to say anything that could come off as mean. (Hey, he was a brother with a car!)

I didn't need any extra light to figure out the problem once I got in and he closed the door, though, because my eyes immediately started to water. Not only was the car packed with stuff, but it smelled like the stairwell of a parking garage or a restroom at a public park—and not one of those nice parks, like in New York City or London, either, you know, where people get engaged and walk their babies. No, this smelled like a restroom at a park where people pee anywhere they feel like it.

So we're driving along to the movie theater and I'm trying to make conversation while I breathe through my mouth, but it's not going well.

"So where do you live?" I say.

"You know, I'm in between apartments right now," Shaqkobe says.

I start putting the pieces together, but he keeps driving along like everything is cool. When someone is between jobs, I'm thinking to myself, *That means they don't have a job*. So if someone is between apartments . . . oh good Lord, *I'm on a date with a homeless man!*

Maybe the Shaqkobe I met at Uncle Andre's was only put together because his brother was there checking up on him, helping him get his stuff together. Maybe the Shaqkobe I met at the grocery store was the *real* Shaqkobe. He wasn't disheveled from being in a hurry like many of us are when we go to the store—he was disheveled from living in his car!

So we get to the movie theater, pick up our tickets, and I can finally relax a little because now I can breathe fresh air and watch a good movie for two hours without having to worry about the pee conversation we'll need to have before we get back in the car and he takes me home.

But first we hit the concession stand. We each order a soda and decide to split a large popcorn. The cashier rings it up, and immediately Shaqkobe starts fumbling around in his pockets looking for his wallet. I've seen guys do this with friends of mine. They try to get out of paying by taking extralong to find their money and hoping that their date will jump in because women are civilized creatures who don't like to hold up lines or make the people around them feel awkward. I wasn't even trying to hear any of that. So I just looked at him. Finally, he takes out his wallet and pulls out a card. It's a Ralph's grocery card. Shaqkobe's trying to pay with Ralph's reward points? Oh no, Shaqkobe's trying not to pay at all.

CAN YOU BELIEVE THAT?!?

Whatever—I'll pay for it, we'll watch the movie, I'll go home, and that'll be that. It's not like I didn't understand what it's like to have no money and need to be extrafrugal.

My dad growing up was so cheap you couldn't even call him frugal—that's too expensive of a word!

Dad was always generous with people, just not with things. Remember the old van we had that his wheelchair flew out the back of? Well, that van also had those little triangle windows in the front doors that you could open in order to adjust the sideview mirrors. At some point, the latch on the driver's-side triangle window broke, so the window would never stay open, and when you drive a van with no air-conditioning and you live in Florida, any kind of closed window is not an option.

The smart thing to do would have been to get it fixed; the *cheap* thing to do was to find something to keep the window propped open. The Mr. Fix-It that he wasn't, my dad found the perfect solution in a half-empty spray can of Right Guard deodorant. I don't know where he found it, but it fit perfectly, and he drove with it in the window for months.

If that wasn't proof enough of his thriftiness, one day he hit a bump on the freeway and the can fell out the window. He stopped the van (this time he was kind enough to pull over to the side of the road) and made me go fetch it. Latches were expensive to fix, and this Right Guard can fit perfectly—who knows if he'd ever be able to find another perfect fit again. I guess if you were willing to let your daughter wander out into the middle of freeway traffic to retrieve your wheelchair, and you grew up in the kind of family where you'd get spanked for asking for an expensive cookie, risking the life of your firstborn for an empty can of deodorant doesn't seem all that unreasonable. And yet, when you take all that into consideration and you think about all the health problems my dad faced, he always bought us popcorn at the movies and our car never smelled like pee.

Which brings me back to Shaqkobe . . . So we're sitting there in the theater, and the movie begins, and who pops up on the screen? Tommy, the famous guy I dated a year earlier. (He's one of the costars.)

Then I smelled something. It was really strong, so strong that I didn't think it could be him. But it never dissipated. *Is that his breath,* I asked myself, *or did he just fart?* In that moment it dawned on me: *OMG, this guy is passing gas, while I watch the guy that I used to date.* (FYI, Tommy ended up being nominated for an Oscar for that movie.) Hollywood ex on the screen, farting homeless man as my date.

This can't be happening. Is this really my life? What did I do in a previous life to deserve this?

The whole time I'm sitting there, breathing through my mouth—AGAIN!—staring at the giant movie screen thinking, *I could've been dating that guy! That guy up there on the screen looking all hot and cool and famous, we could be together right now. Instead, I'm stuck in this dark theater with a homeless*

flatulation machine, and about to get a ride home in his pee
mobile.

I decided right then and there: I'm done with black guys!
I'm kidding, of course—I just needed to expand my dating
horizons beyond random guys at the club, or comedy club
guys, or guys who I met on line in a store. None of them had
what I felt like I needed.

It was just a coincidence that the next man I dated was an
older white guy from church whom I called "PK" because he
was a preacher's kid. He reminded me of the character Jethro
Bodine from the old TV show *The Beverly Hillbillies*. He was
cute and strong and kind of simple. That was okay, though.
I couldn't work with *stank* or stupid, but I could work with
simple.

My main concern though wasn't whether *I* could make it
work, it was whether other people could.

Surprise, surprise, my mom had very strange opinions
about black and white for as long as I could remember. For

instance, she hated when I used to dip my chocolate chip cookies in milk.

"Why you gotta dunk those cookies in that white milk!?" she'd say every time she caught me doing it. She said it so often it eventually gave me a complex. In college, I'd turn the lights off in my room and crawl under the covers any time I wanted to have cookies and milk.

One day, when I was really young, we went to an ice cream shop for a treat, and my mom told DeOnzell and me that we could get whatever we wanted. The freezers were full of all these exotic flavors: mocha almond fudge, pralines 'n' cream, strawberry shortcake, mint chip, rainbow sherbet. I went from one end to the other considering each flavor until I finally made a decision.

"I want vanilla," I said.

"Vanilla! VA-NIL-LA!" she repeated slowly. My mom looked at me like I'd just spit on the grave of Martin Luther King Jr. I didn't know that's why she was upset at the time, however—I thought she was bothered by my manners.

"Sorry, Mom," I said, then turned to the man behind the counter and asked very respectfully, "May I have vanilla, *please?*"

My mom was beside herself. Of all these flavors, her daughter had to pick vanilla. She and my dad did not endure decades of discrimination and work their behinds off to raise a daughter who ordered *vanilla*! Seeing her frustration, I quickly changed my mind and ordered bubble gum instead, since it had the most colors in it. That made her happy.

I brought this story up to my mom recently and we both laughed about it. I said, "You know, Mom, vanilla actually comes from a bean that is black."

She didn't miss a beat.

"Yes, and the only way people will eat it is if you slit it open, scrape out its insides, and then whip it with milk and sugar until it's white."

I wasn't going to argue. God bless that woman.

To my mother's credit, while she certainly was different, she wasn't discriminatory. She was totally fine with my white boyfriend PK. She was happy if I was happy.

And I was. Until the wheels came off, that is.

It started with PK's bathroom habits. We'd go to a restaurant for dinner, have a wonderful meal—even better conversation—and then, when he was finished with his food, he'd go to the bathroom and disappear for twenty, thirty, *forty* minutes. The first time it happened I was worried that he may have gotten himself locked in, or that he had fallen into the toilet and got stuck. Then he'd come out and act like nothing happened.

When we were by ourselves, this weirdness was bad enough, but when we were around other people, well, that's when it got *really* uncomfortable.

A couple weeks into dating, we went over to my friends' house to watch a movie. A bunch of us were hanging out, not doing much of anything, when sure enough, he excuses himself to go to the bathroom. When the door closes, my friends give him the thumbs-up.

"We like him!"

"He's a great conversationalist."

"He seems to be a couple french fries short of a happy meal, but he's sweet. . . ."

And I'm, like, yes, yes, and yes. . . .

And then thirty minutes go by, then forty, then an hour, then another fifteen minutes, and still he doesn't come out of the bathroom. My friends' opinions turn on a dime.

"We don't like him!"

"What is he doing in there?"

"Does he know how to turn a doorknob?"

When PK finally emerged from his cocoon like a bathroom butterfly, one of my friends got up slyly a couple minutes after and went into the bathroom to do some reconnaissance. She didn't find anything. It didn't smell. The toilet didn't look like it had been flushed, the sink basin wasn't wet, the toilet paper roll was full, the hand towels were dry, nothing was missing from the medicine cabinet.

To this day none of us can figure out what he was doing that whole time in the bathroom—or any time in the bathroom for that matter. Was he praying? Doing drugs? Texting another girl? It was, and it remains, a complete mystery.

Still, I defended him. My list of important character traits in a boyfriend had shrunk so far by this point—he was cute, he had a job, he didn't stink, he had his own place where his family didn't live—I could handle some weird bathroom habits.

The deal breaker came shortly after this when he took me for lunch one day to a restaurant called Souplantation. I'd never heard of Souplantation before this moment. If you've never heard of Souplantation, either, it's a chain restaurant that serves, *duh*, soup. When we pulled up in front of it, I looked at PK like he was crazy. Does he really think I'm stepping one foot inside a restaurant with "plantation" in its name?

You probably think that sounds crazy, and I understand especially if you're on the younger side, but you have to realize where I come from, with a mother who has opinions on black-white relations that go all the way down to the level of dessert, that there was no way I was going to cross her when it came to *lunch!*

Do you want to know who I bet *wouldn't* be surprised by my reaction? SOUPLANTATION! Because in the South, that company doesn't call its restaurants "Souplantation," it calls them "Sweet Tomatoes."

It's not uncommon for a franchise to have different names depending on where you are in the country. Like Biggie and Tupac, there's an East Coast / West Coast thing. Carl's Jr. in California is Hardee's in Florida. Best Foods mayonnaise is Hellman's (that's what we used on Patrice). Dreyer's ice cream is Edy's. The difference between all those companies, though, is that *only one of them uses a different name to avoid making a whole lot of African Americans really upset.*

This was my first experience dating anyone outside my race, so I knew we'd bump into cultural differences eventually. I just never expected it to involve a piping hot bowl of Yankee Clipper clam chowder. As a black woman from the South, I had a serious problem with this, but PK didn't understand. I mean he "got it," the way you understand that racism is bad, but he didn't really *get it* the way you do when you try to understand how someone else might feel. This was the simple part of PK finally biting me in the rump, and I couldn't work with it after all.

What was it going to take to find a good guy? I didn't *need* a man in my life—I never have, and you don't either, by the way—but I wanted a partner to share my journey with.

It felt like God was punishing me—for not being a good wife, for getting divorced, for not keeping my hands inside the ride at all times when Jacqui and I were Rogue and Storm, who knows? All I know is that this string of guys would have tested even the most trusting person's faith in humanity.

A couple months after I broke up with PK, I flew back to Orlando to get away from everything and to help my mom pass out flyers for Congresswoman Corrine Brown (the representative of Florida's Fifth Congressional District) at the annual Zora Neale Hurston Festival in Eatonville, Florida. It's a weeklong event, which is too much flyering for any sane person, so I came in on the second or third day to meet up with my mom and help her out. I walk into her house and she's getting all dressed up—way too dressed up to stand out in the Florida heat passing out flyers.

"Mom, are you going to the festival?"

"Oh no, I can't go to the festival today. I've got to go to my prayer meeting."

Mom should have used air quotes when she said "prayer meeting" because all that meant was that she was going to play cards with a bunch of little old ladies from church.

"I came to visit you and spend time with you, now you're going to play cards and I'm stuck passing out flyers by myself?" I was so annoyed. Is everyone going to make promises to me and not deliver? Is everything going to seem one way, but be another?

"No, baby, you won't be by yourself," Mom said, like she knew what would make me feel better. "You're going with Ms.

Sanders. Her daughter works for Congresswoman Brown. You can take her car."

Ms. Sanders is a very loud, brassy, say-what's-on-my-mind-because-I'm-old-enough-to-get-away-with-anything kind of person. She also used to be the lunch lady at Jones High School when my father was a student there and would always give him extra food because she could tell he was hungry. For the wake after his funeral, she even brought his favorite meal—Mexican meat pie. Of course I would happily drive her to the festival, even if I would less happily pass out flyers by myself.

So there I am at the Zora Neale Hurston Festival, and it's hot, and there's no place to sit down, and I'm trying to get the attention of people who are more interested in looking for deals on shea butter. It couldn't get any worse if I was at a drive-through window architecture conference inside a Souplantation that smelled like pee and onion farts!

I walk around a little while longer and I come across this ring of bricks that looks like it was created to cover up an old well. People had started to sit on it while they ate food from the refreshment tents, and there was one spot left, so I took it. It was no La-Z-Boy recliner, but it was the most comfortable I'd been in hours. I said to myself, *You know what, I'm just gonna pass out my flyers from here,* and that's what I did. I didn't get up until I ran out of flyers and had to go back to the congresswoman's tent where they had extras.

When I returned not two minutes later, there was a man in my seat. I was *not* having it. I was, like, *This man has got-ta move!* I'd had it with men. They were either lying mama's boys, or stanky homeless, or IHOP-ordering big timers, or they didn't get why *plantation* was a bad word. I was not about to let this brother take my seat. I had an attitude, I didn't care. I was at my wit's end.

"Don't you want to meet your congresswoman," I said to him. It was not a question, it was an accusation.

He barely looked up and said, simply, "No."

Okay, then. I had to figure something out quickly here, because it was hot and my goal was to get him up out of that seat. If I had to bug him or threaten him, I was going to do it.

I'm exasperated, so I take a step back to look him over. He had his head down, and I could tell he didn't have a girlfriend or a wife because there was no ring on his finger and there was no way a woman would have let him out of the house the way he was dressed. He wasn't a raggedy mess, like Shaqkobe, but his stuff wasn't put together the way it could have been. Then he started talking.

"So do you work here or something? What do you do?" Oh, now Mr. Cement Cheeks thinks he can ask me all sorts of questions?

"I'm a comedian," I reluctantly said. "I live in Los Angeles."

"I like comedians," he says, and finally looks up at me as he scoots over a little on the bricks. I squished in next to him, practically on his lap.

The next thing I know, it's five hours later, and we haven't stopped talking once. People are coming up to us saying, *Y'all make such a cute couple,* and I'm, like, "I don't even know this man!"

His name was Kevin Simon. He was an engineer and a retired sergeant in the U.S. Air Force who had just moved back to Florida after a divorce from his wife to be near his last living parent—his dad.

Eventually, it was time to go. Ms. Sanders wanted to head back and hang out with her friends after they got home from their "prayer meeting." On the ride home, I told her about this man I had just met. She told me if I dropped her off at the house, I could use the car to go out to dinner with him as long as I returned it to her at the end of the night. I was grateful; it was very kind of her.

SK and I went to dinner that night, and again we talked for hours. It was a long night, and it was late when I finally returned the car. SK followed me to Ms. Sanders's house in his car so he could give me a ride home. We pull up happy and excited about this connection that was building quickly, only to find two squad cars in her driveway and two police officers in her living room. Ms. Sanders had called the police and reported the car stolen, knowing full well I had it! I was completely embarrassed. How do you tell the police, in front of your new bae, that the old lady who used to take care of her dad was losing her marbles? I knew that if SK still wanted to talk to me after this, things were probably going to work out between us.

I went back to Los Angeles a couple days later, and wouldn't you know it, we kept on talking. I still had my blog back then, so I would write about him, telling my readers all about this new guy I met named Kevin and how special he was. I started calling him "Special K" because I like giving people nicknames, which I quickly shortened even further to "SK" because I'm lazy when it comes to writing.

I still had plenty of attitude with him, don't be mistaken. I hadn't gone head over heels, like I might have when I was younger. It was more, like, "I live in California, I'm not moving back to Florida, no matter how special you are." SK was cool with that—he understood what I was trying to do out here, and we agreed to start visiting each other.

When I visited SK the very first time, I could tell he wasn't really feeling Florida. His dad had remarried and was doing his own thing, and he still didn't have that many friends in Orlando, which left him to just sort of twiddle his thumbs between his workday and our conversations on the phone.

Before I left to go back to Los Angeles I casually said, "You know, you should move out to California." I didn't exactly mean move to California *with me* . . . but that's what ended up happening. SK came out to Los Angeles, moved in with me in my tiny, not-even-a-one-bedroom guesthouse attached to the owner's garage, and we started dating IRL.

———————

It was a modern-day fairy tale except instead of living in a castle, the princess lived off the garage of another house, and instead of a luxurious four-poster bed, she slept on the floor and cooked on a hot plate.

Still, we made it work, despite the difficulty SK had in finding work. It was the middle of the Great Recession, and good jobs were hard to come by. That didn't stop him, though—SK took a job as a bagger at the Veterans Administration store to help pay rent and bills, and it wasn't just to carry his own weight. It also helped me as I continued to pursue my entertainment dreams.

It would be another couple years before I got traction on YouTube, started making good money, and then made myself the number one person in my life (instead of Jacqui) in order to focus on our relationship, but those early days were when I knew SK was truly special.

Now you might be asking yourself: *GloZell, these stories are great, and I'm very happy for you* (thank you, by the way) *but why are you telling us all of this? What's the point?*

The point is that God wasn't punishing me for any kind of sin by putting me through the ringer with this string of crazy guys before I met SK. Those relationships weren't a test of my faith (at least not in God, maybe in *myself*), they were just a part of life. Even when you feel like you're doing everything right, things aren't always going to go your way. You're going to have some misses. You're going to want some do-overs. Unfortunately, that's not how life works. You don't get do-overs. Instead, what you get is the ability to learn from your mistakes.

I firmly believe that everything happens for a reason. I believe you attract what comes into your life, good and bad. In both good and bad moments—but especially in bad ones— the key is that you learn from those mistakes so you don't repeat them. This is most important when it comes to your relationships, because identifying and learning from those mistakes helps you figure out what you definitely don't want in your life and what you absolutely have to have.

My relationships with Dwayne, Tommy, Shaqkobe, and PK led me to SK. They taught me that I didn't want a liar or a mama's boy. They showed me that I couldn't be with someone who also had a big personality and might make me change in his shadow. They confirmed my suspicions that homeless cheapskates living in pee mobiles weren't for me. And they made me realize that I would have a hard time with someone who didn't understand my experiences or what made me different.

They taught me that what I absolutely had to have was a strong, honest, independent man (with no mama! *LOL*), who was most interested in supporting me on my journey instead of overshadowing it, who was self-sufficient and self-confident, and who understood where I came from and where I was going.

My bad relationships set the path that led to SK. Being willing to learn from my mistakes opened that path in front of me. Knowing who I was and having faith in myself gave me the courage to walk it.

You are going to have a lot of moments in your life like I had on the phone with Dwayne, or in the movie theater with Shaqkobe, or in the car outside Souplantation with PK. Yours might not be related to boys or girls. They might be school or work or family related. They might be on Facebook or Snapchat or Instagram or in the comments to one of your YouTube videos. They're going to feel like big mistakes or failures. Many of them are going to feel like they're your fault, even when they're not.

Your job is not to pretend that those moments aren't hard, or that they don't make you feel bad. You're not a robot, you're a person. Your job is to embrace your true self, remember that you're the number one person in your life, and learn from these mistakes. Learn what's important to you and what isn't, what you never want to repeat, and what you need.

If you can learn to do those things, you will always find a way back onto your path toward a long, happy life, because you will be doing the things you love, with the people you care about. I can't promise it will be easy or immediate, but I promise it will happen.

CHAPTER 10

STAND OUT TO BREAK OUT

Q: Why do you wear green? What is your favorite shade of green?

A: I wear green because my last name is Green. If my last name was "Neonpink" I'd wear neon pink, then I'd ask my mom where we're from because that's a ridiculous last name. I like lighter greens, not Kelly green, or forest green, or Kermit green. More like a tea green, or chartreuse.

———————————

My career as a YouTuber began unintentionally—I definitely didn't set out to become a viral video star, or an online personality, or whatever term people use today to describe those of us who create on the Internet.

At first, YouTube was just a tool for my blog, an easier way to host videos than having to do it myself. Then it became a vehicle to keep me sane after *The Tonight Show* kicked me out—the best way I knew to express myself without any restrictions or boundaries. When I got my feet under me, YouTube then became a kind of rehearsal space for my sitcom ideas, until finally it became my path to entertainment success.

It's funny how stuff like that works in life. You take a chance on something, you sign up for something not even thinking about it, and then, *BAM*, it's a huge part of your life every day for years and years. That's a good reason to take chances and put yourself out there by the way. You never know what might happen.

I owe a lot to YouTube in that regard, more than I can ever repay. Oddly though, the one thing I don't actually think I owe to it is my success. Before you get mad, and think I'm throwing shade, let me explain what I mean.

YouTube gave me the platform to be successful, and the company's invaluable support (and unlimited bandwidth!) over the years helped me build on that success, but the website was not the *reason* I became successful. The real secret ingredient was something else, something inside of me, something that's inside any of us really: *the willingness to stand out.*

I truly believe that if I had not tried to stand out, I'd be just another person posting videos, and my videos would be just another collection of four-minute snippets from some random person's life.

Think about the numbers: by the end of 2014, there were three hundred hours of video being uploaded to YouTube *every minute*. That was three times as much as the year before. Today? If I didn't stand out? I'd barely be a tiny squeak in an ocean of voices. I don't mean that as an insult or in a negative, diminishing way, to anyone who posts videos for fun. I think everyone who wants to make videos should make as many as they can and post them as often as they want. But there is a difference between using something like YouTube to figure out who you are and what you want to say on the one hand, and then going out and being successful at it on the other. To me, that difference will always be the willingness and ability to stand out.

What does it mean to stand out? Most people think it means being different from everyone else. I don't think that's it, though. Being different isn't something you *do*, it's something you *are*. You can't *control* being different, and being different certainly isn't up to you. I had no say in who my parents were or where I went to school, so I had very little influence over how those two things impacted who I became as a person. If all it took to stand out was *being* different, then wouldn't success become sort of a lottery? We'd be saying that only certain *types* of people can be successful on a place like YouTube. You either have "it" or you don't.

Not only is that unfair, I believe it's untrue. Anyone can be successful. The world is full of Plain Janes and Average Joes with talent or something to say, and what is holding them back isn't that they're "like everybody else," it's that they haven't learned how to use their talent or their message to stand out.

Just take the singer Adele. Adele is an average-looking, average-shaped white woman from a middle-class family in South London. If you saw her walking down the street in 2006, you'd say "there goes an average young woman," if you even noticed her in the first place.

To hear Adele sing, though, there is nothing average about that at all. That huge viral video from the BBC when she auditioned in disguise as an Adele impersonator is a perfect example. There she was, amid all these singers who either dressed or tried to look just like her, and the second she opened her mouth, stand-out genius talent flew out. She has a voice like God stuffed a choir of angels down her throat and then turned the dial up to 11. She hits notes that hit you in the heart and the soul and the mind and the spirit, all at once.

But talk to any music industry person or any of the judges on *American Idol* or *X Factor*, and they'll tell you that talent isn't enough to be really successful in their business. It never is. You have to stand out in other ways. For Adele, that had to be easier said than done. Just look at all the artists "like her" who were putting out major albums around the same time she was ready to release her first major studio album in 2008: Taylor Swift, Katy Perry, Fergie, Lady Gaga, Carrie Underwood, Ke$ha. How do you stand out in a group like that? I'd be freaking out if I were her. I'd be, like, "Okay, so I have to dress like Effie from *Hunger Games* but I have to sing like Christina Aguilera from the *Moulin Rouge* soundtrack, and I have to tour like a one-woman Cirque du Soleil show." The thing is, if she had done that, she wouldn't have stood out at all; she would have blended right in alongside what Gaga and Katy Perry and Rihanna and Taylor Swift were doing.

Smartly, Adele went the other way. She went simple. She sang songs that were about things going on in her relationship and made an album whose title was just a number (*19*)—her age when she made the album. And instead of big stadium concerts with dancers and fireworks and giant screens, it was just her and a simple backing band in a theater big enough to let her voice fill the room, but still small enough for you to see her from the back row as she blows your hair back from the front of the stage. I don't know any of them, but I bet Adele as a person and an artist isn't so different from the Taylor Swifts and the Carrie Underwoods of the music world. Yet in 2008 (and beyond) she did something totally different from all of them, and the results since then have been undeniable: her second album, *21*, set a bunch of records; and her third album, *25*, sold more copies in its first week than any other album in the history of music.

All because she stood out.

It took me years to figure this out—that if you really want to break out, you have to stand out first. I think it was because for most of the time after I arrived in California, I wasn't trying to break out, I was trying to *break in*—to stand-up comedy, to *The Tonight Show*, to television in general. I was trying to be discovered instead of trying to be distinct. I actually remember the exact day I started to get it.

———————————

The day I worked it out was January 30, 2012. The day I did the Cinnamon Challenge.

The Cinnamon Challenge was not my idea—not the concept, or the desire to do it. Both the concept and the desire came from my fans.

I love connecting with my fans. I've been communicating with them since I started my *glozelllovesjayleno* blog in 2006, right from the very first comment someone posted to one of my blog entries. When I moved over to YouTube full-time in 2008, most of the readers from the blog shifted over with me, and we picked up right where we left off, growing the community together.

As my channel got bigger and bigger—first with the Push-Up Bra video and the Hair Removal video, then a year later with my original song about the lady with stank breath—it got more difficult to stay connected to everyone. On top of that, I was losing myself inside "Project Jacqui" a little, so I didn't spend as much time engaging with my fans as I could or should have. That all changed in the second half of 2011 when I ghosted from Jacqui and then recommitted to my channel, and to myself.

Up until then, I had never taken suggestions from my fans for things to do in my videos. I was using YouTube as a playground for sketches, characters, and ideas that I might be able to use one day when I got my own show, so it didn't make sense to me to go to the comments section of my channel for ideas. But once I did—once I reengaged with the most die-hard of my fans—I was amazed by what I found: a huge audience that had unique tastes, and very specific things they wanted to see. They were like my own little focus group, except not so little. If I listened to them, it could be like having my ear to the ground as the viral train came roaring down the tracks.

The Cinnamon Challenge was the first train to pull into GloZell Station. My fans hounded me for months to do it, sending me links to other YouTubers doing it, blowing up my Facebook fan page and the comments section to previous videos, like I needed to catch up or something.

"GloZell, you should do the Cinnamon Challenge!"

"GloZell, why haven't you done the Cinnamon Challenge?"

"GlooooooZeeeeeeeellll! Cinnamon Cinnamon Cinnamon Cinnamon Cinnamon! k thx."

"GloZell I am Prince Agabi of Nigeria and I am in prison and need your bank account number so I can give you my money.' (Okay, maybe this one was spam. But he sounds nice. And he *is* royalty!)

As someone whose purpose is to make people laugh and be happy, I understood what the Cinnamon Challenge was about, and even why someone would like to watch videos of it. As a performer, though, I just didn't see the appeal. You grab some ground cinnamon out of the cupboard, you pour some into a teaspoon, and you try to swallow it without coughing it up. Big whoop. Where's the fun in that? Plus, if everybody's already done their version of it, why would anyone watch mine?

If I was going to do this, one of the three elements of the challenge was going to have to change:

The form: powder

The spice: cinnamon

The size: a teaspoon

Let's take these options one at a time.

The only other form cinnamon comes in is its natural form— as a stick, from the bark of a cinnamon tree. I could have eaten that, I guess, but I figured that part of the challenge relates to the cinnamon being in its ground, powdery form. Watching someone chew a stick is boring. Plus, I had a personal rule against eating anything you might find in bathroom potpourri, especially after my experiences with PK. So it had to be powder.

I suppose I could have put my own twist on things by using a different spice altogether—say, turmeric or cumin—but I'm scared of any spices related to Indian food. I love Indian food, it's delicious, but turmeric makes it look like what comes out of a baby's behind, and cumin is what makes it *smell* like it comes out of a baby's behind. Even if I could choke those down, it wouldn't be the *Cinnamon* Challenge. It's called the "Cinnamon Challenge," not the "Baby Tushy Spice Challenge." So it had to be cinnamon.

That left me with the size. So what's bigger than a teaspoon? It turns out pretty much every other standard household measurement is bigger than a teaspoon. Great, that's no help. I thought about doing a tablespoon, but that's just a triple teaspoon, so it didn't seem very interesting. I played around with ounces, but it got confusing after a while because ounces are both a unit of weight and a unit of volume and I didn't have a scale or a measuring cup small enough for either. I could do a cup, I thought, but who has a *cup* of cinnamon lying around the house? Can you even buy cinnamon by the cup?

Finally, I realized I had to flip it. Instead of focusing on measurement size, maybe I needed to pay more attention to *utensil* size. All my utensils could handle one teaspoon of cinnamon, but how many utensils could handle all my teaspoons of cinnamon? Why fiddle around with one versus two versus three teaspoons, when you can just rip off the lid and go wild?

The biggest thing in my kitchen without any holes in it was a four-ounce ladle. Ladles and cinnamon must be a match made in heaven, because guess what size jar of cinnamon they had at Target: 4.1 ounces. Ladle it is.

Remember that old playground rhyme that starts, "First is the worst, second is the best?" That might as well describe my first two challenge videos, because Diet Coke and Mentos (which featured in my second challenge video) are fizzy and delicious, but a ladle full of cinnamon nearly killed me.

I'm not kidding. When the saliva in my mouth made contact with all that cinnamon, it caked up into a paste that clogged my throat and nearly choked me to death. SK was there and acted quickly, so I was okay, but my voice has never been the same since. You know how when I cough it sounds like a frog doing a pig impression? That's from the Cinnamon Challenge.

What little of the cinnamon didn't cement my throat shut managed to explode out of my mouth, much like the video did out onto the Internet. Within days, it had millions of views and was shared all over the place. I was getting interview requests, and websites were writing about me. Sure, ground cinnamon nearly put me in the ground, but it also set me on a new path with challenge videos over the next couple years and officially launched me as a YouTube "star" (however you want to define that). Google even reached out to talk to me about how I could get paid for doing these videos. At 3:03 in length, with 47 million views, that's more than 140,000,000 minutes of viewing time, which is more than 270 *years*. That's longer than the United States has been a country. I should be able to get at least a hundred bucks out of that! *Cha-ching.*

I'm still amazed when I think back to those days. Hundreds of people had done the Cinnamon Challenge before me; how was I the one to break out because of it? Well, I think the answer is pretty obvious at this point: it's because I did something different, and I stood out as a result. Just like Adele went smaller and simpler and it worked for her, I went bigger and crazier, and it worked for me.

Going forward I applied the same principle to pretty much every challenge video, song parody, and collab I did. When I took photos with fans or celebrities, I took a page out of Jay Leno's book from back in the day and posed with my mouth open—except I took it to the extreme. My philosophy was "go big or stay home."

When I did the Salt & Ice Challenge—where you sprinkle salt on your skin, set ice cubes on top of it, and see how long you can hold it there before it gets too painful—I dumped half a canister of table salt the length of my arm and covered it in ice cubes. I didn't last very long and it nearly gave me frostbite, but I got fourteen million views (as well as a few cute skin burns) out of it.

When I did the Saltine Challenge—the one where you try to eat six saltine crackers in a minute—I felt like that was too easy, so I put peanut butter on them and then handcuffed my hands behind my back.

When I did any challenge involving hot things—peppers, sauce, wasabi—the question was never whether I could handle it, it was always whether I could fit *all of it* in my mouth at once. (FYI, the answer was usually no.)

Google has something called the "10x philosophy." They don't want to do things ten *percent* better than the competition, they want to do it ten *times* better, because that's how you become wildly successful.

So it was with me. If I was going to make that paper like Google promised I could, I needed to keep standing out, and going big was going to be my strategy. It was how I would differentiate myself from other video creators who were doing similar things competing for the attention of a lot of the same audiences (there are only so many eyeballs and so many hours in the day, after all). My YouTube friends were all young, sparkly little beauties doing their own thing, so I needed to have a thing of my own.

———————————

Mark Twain—the author of *Tom Sawyer* and *The Adventures of Huckleberry Finn*—wrote something great about how to live a good, unique life: "Whenever you find yourself on the side of the majority, it's time to pause and reflect." My philosophy is similar: *When everyone else is doing it one way, do it the other. Do you, not them.*

What's funny about that is while it took me several years to figure out the importance of standing out and doing *you*, it took me even longer to realize that I had actually been doing it the entire time I'd been in Los Angeles.

As a stand-up comedian, I was 100 percent clean, while nearly everyone around me was dirty. My jokes were family-friendly, their jokes were like an episode of *Empire*. I brought in a whole new crowd to the comedy clubs where I performed, while the other comics served the same audience everywhere they went. Ultimately, I decided that stand-up comedy wasn't for me. But here's the thing: I made that decision *after* three years of doing stand-up, performing at every famous club in Los Angeles and a few in New York City. And don't forget—I'd started in my thirties, when everyone told me I was too late. I succeeded not because I was better than all the other comics (I wasn't). I made a living because I stood out. I did something different.

When I moved along to *The Tonight Show*, I *literally* stood out. As in, I stood outside every day and talked to people. Plenty of folks who looked like me have come and gone from *Tonight Show* audiences over the years without ever being noticed. Not me. I was doing something different. It wasn't bigger and crazier like my challenge videos would be, but it was *more* and . . . okay . . . maybe crazier. I went every day, all day. That's what caught the attention of the pages, who suggested I start a blog. Overnight I went from an audience *in line*, to an audience *online*.

Already in 2006, there were millions of blogs out there. Why did mine find a readership, while so many other bloggers struggled to even get their friends to read their stuff? I think it's because I was doing something nobody had ever done before on the Internet: I was providing a behind-the-scenes look at what it's like to go watch a taping of a late-night talk show that has been broadcast into every home in America for more than sixty years.

When I switched over to YouTube in 2008, the site was still very young. Nobody had really figured out what potential it held for entertainers, yet I quickly built a following there, and one of the big reasons was that I was obsessed with posting videos. I posted every day, sometimes multiple times per day. More often than not the videos weren't very interesting or they were poor quality, but it wasn't the quality that people were judging at that point, it was the consistency. I didn't mean to be, but I kind of became one of the first daily vloggers. Very few people were doing things like that, so naturally my channel stood out.

My very first meet and greet was in a frozen yogurt store across the street from my apartment in Studio City. I know what you're thinking: *That's a weird place to have a meet and greet.* EXACTLY! Casey Neistat once did one at a Dollar Pizza shop in New York. It wouldn't make any sense if *I'd* done one there, but it made perfect sense to him and his YouTube fans.

One summer, SK and I wanted to get out of L.A. for a while, so we packed up our car and decided to drive cross-country to Florida to visit our families. Along the way I figured, why not turn this trip into an impromptu tour? So every town we pulled into for gas, or for lunch or to stay the night, I would announce where I was, pick a place that had a decent amount of space and was free to get into, and within an hour a bunch of fans would show up. You want to know some of the places I held these events? Subway; Golden Corral; Target (I loved Targets, they're *huge*); a Flying J's truck stop. It was amazing. The appearances cost nothing to put on, everybody had a great time, I got to meet some spectacular, die-hard fans, and we all walked away with memories that will last forever. Not to mention free food at some places. I mean, who would ever forget meeting a perfect stranger on a whim at a truck stop outside of Lake Charles, Louisiana, where you also got a free churro? I know I haven't.

I even chose my green lipstick specifically to stand out, though probably not in the way you think.

I started wearing the green lipstick when I was out in public because I was getting recognized more and more, but by kids who weren't sure it was actually me. They'd stare at me from a distance, or circle me at the mall, or follow me down the aisles of the grocery store. Some of them I'm sure were just shy, but others I could tell were with parents who were worried their kid might seem racist for going up to a random black woman assuming she must be someone famous. *For the last time, girl, I am NOT Beyoncé!* I wanted to make it easier on them, and make them feel comfortable coming up to say hi, so I wore the green lipstick as a signal. Green means Go Ahead.

It turns out I didn't need to find my own thing, I had it the entire time. I just needed to recognize it and lean into it. The

Cinnamon Challenge video was the first time I really did that. It was the first video where I was conscious of standing out and differentiating myself. I think what gave me the confidence to go out on a limb like that was the long track record of standing out that I had unwittingly established almost from the minute I pulled into Los Angeles in 2003. When I was learning to play the piano, my mom always said that practice makes perfect. I guess that idea is not just limited to playing an instrument, or participating in a sport, because it seems like the more I practiced at standing out, the better I got at it, until finally the willingness to stand out led to the ability to break out.

If you're a young person reading this, I want you to know that I understand if you feel like the idea of standing out is really scary and difficult. When you're young and you feel different, the last thing you ever want to do is stand out. You want to fit in with your classmates and friends and neighborhood kids. I know I did, and that's okay. Don't worry about standing out just yet. You focus your courage on understanding what makes you different, why that difference is okay, and then accepting your true self for who she or he is.

Your time to shine will come soon enough.

Just know that as you get older, the value of blending in will decrease, and the importance of standing out will increase.

That doesn't mean you should try to change who you are. If you are a Plain Jane or an Average Joe, that's great, you should embrace it. It's not *who* or *what* you are that is the difference, after all, it's what you *do*. It's not necessarily the talent or the message itself, it's how you put it out into the world, and how you present yourself to the people you want to reach.

When my mom made those crazy church crowns for GloZell Fest in 2014, the idea itself was a reflection of how different she is from your average mom. What made the hats stand out was their spectacular construction and her decision not just to put them on a table by the side of the stage, but to have them modeled in an impromptu fashion show by my YouTuber friends and fans. In that moment, none of them could believe it was happening. And as a result, when someone says, "I can't believe this is happening right now!," what they're really saying is, "I'm never going to forget this." That's why they still ask about those hats. Of all the things we've done together, those hats are one of the things that most stand out.

Now, not everyone wants to break out. A lot of people don't believe they have big things to achieve. Some people prefer just to go along to get along and lead a quiet, humble life. Doing what I have done isn't for everybody, I get it.

Still, there is no reason you can't be one of the people who stands out in whatever you choose to do, whether it's in school or with your dreams, in life, or in your career. I am living proof that it doesn't matter when or where or how you start; all that matters is that you try. And if you stand out long enough, the potential to break out gets closer to 100 percent with each passing day.

YOU IS OKAY. YOU IS.

When SK and I got married in 2013, we started talking about having a baby right away. I was forty-one years old, which is on the older side to have your first child, but not so old that anyone, least of all SK and I, thought it was impossible.

Our doctors were with us, and we tried everything. Prayers, crystals, diet, massage, shots, vitamins, ointments, acupuncture—the list goes on. There's nothing I didn't try. You name it—if the Internet said it boosted fertility, or aided in conception, we tried it at least once. We went about trying to have a baby like this for several years, with no luck. All we got was pain, and disappointment, and a lot of tears.

I had faith that I was on the right path, that everything happening to us was happening for a reason, but each time it didn't happen, it just felt like a giant slap in the face.

I'd struggled for years—*decades*, really—to achieve what
I have in entertainment. I fought and hustled beyond the
expectations of nearly everyone I came up against. I made
sure to learn from all my mistakes—finally, I had put them
in the rearview mirror and forged ahead.

But in my efforts to get pregnant I began wondering if it was
all worth it. Does any of this effort mean anything if you
don't have someone to pass your legacy on to? All my friends
kept telling me that plenty of women had children in their
forties: Halle Berry, Gwen Stefani, Celine Dion, Tina Fey.
There had to be something we could do.

———————

Finally, SK and I admitted to ourselves that something else
had to be done. We needed help beyond what the two of us
and our doctors could provide.

We needed a surrogate.

This was not an easy decision. For thirty years, I'd relied
almost entirely on myself to get where I was. I had trouble
trusting or opening up to more than one person at a time,
and now I was supposed to put all my trust and faith in a
woman I'd never met? If you'd asked me a year ago, "is you
okay?" with this option, I would have said, "is you crazy?!"

In the first months of 2015, SK and I interviewed a handful of wonderful women through an agency called "Gifted Journeys," with the help of our surrogacy adviser, Wendie Wilson-Miller. As hard as our entire fertility journey had been, these interviews and meetings were some of the most difficult things we faced. This was a huge decision for everyone involved—we were trusting another person to bring our child into the world, and that person was agreeing to basically rent us her body for a year. It's about as intimate a bond as you can create with a perfect stranger.

In April, SK and I found our surrogate. Her name is Shawna. She is amazing. She's more than amazing actually; she's an angel. She's taken such great care of our baby and herself, and she's been so gracious and open about sharing our journey together with all of you.

When Shawna agreed to do this for us and we started the process, something came over me. I felt this irrepressible need to write a book. I didn't know about what yet, but I knew there was a story that had to come out of me before our baby came out of her.

My YouTube channel had taken off in the previous three years in large part because of my challenge videos, so I knew they'd be part of my story. The other, more personal, component of the book was less clear. Then I started thinking about some of my stories from growing up in Florida. It became apparent pretty quickly, even to me, that I had faced some unique challenges that other people might be able to learn from.

In December, thanks to Dr. Kolb at HRC Pasadena, SK and I got our wish. The implantation procedure had been successful, and Shawna was pregnant. It was the happiest day of our lives. It was the day SK and I had been hoping for and struggling to get to for longer than I can even remember. We were going to bring a new life into this world. I was going to be a mom.

In that moment, I knew what this book needed to be about.

For years, my video creator friends have called me "the mother of the Internet." Usually I just laughed it off—though I was honored they would think of me that way, it was still a silly title. No one person birthed and raised the Internet. It was a group effort. Like my bestie Hillary Clinton once said, "It takes a village." Letting the news of our pregnancy sink in, I sat there thinking about the fact that in nine months I would be responsible for raising a child and equipping him or her with the tools to be happy, healthy, and successful. It is a big job, and up until that moment I honestly had no idea how I was going to feel about it. When I learned that I wouldn't be able to carry our baby, I thought the moment might be difficult. Instead, I felt something completely different: a sense of comfort and familiarity.

I realized that I was already in a very similar position with most of my fans and many of my collaborators on YouTube, Vine, and Snapchat. I was twenty, sometimes thirty years older than many of my "colleagues." I had so much experience, so much life wisdom, so many lessons learned just sitting inside of me that I was bursting at the seams to share with them, which I never had. That was the book I needed to write.

Writing the book, I realized that the lessons from my life stories weren't just for preteen girls and boys or aspiring YouTubers or new moms like we originally thought. I like to think that they are universal; they apply to everyone. I hope that when you string them together, you'll find that they are like a philosophy that anyone can use to figure out how to accept their true selves, find their path, find their friends, love their family, and be successful in whatever they do, however they define it.

As I sit here, despite all my scared skepticism and early self-doubt, I recognize that my fertility journey was not an exception to the lessons I discovered as I wrote this book—it was the product of them.

I'm different. I made different choices. I had to find my true self to figure out if I really wanted to have a baby. And if I did, I had to accept that there were no excuses. I had to do whatever needed to be done to make it happen, no matter how old I was. As long as I had faith, as long as I was open to the paths that opened themselves to me, as long as I put SK and myself first in our lives, we could overcome every misstep and false start we encountered.

My path has been a bumpy and winding road, with many pitfalls along the way. My hope is that this book will help you avoid some of those obstacles on your journey. My dream is that you can take advantage of its lessons to get a jump on happiness. Because life doesn't have to just be okay. I promise, it can be great.

GloZell Green
February 14, 2016
(Happy Valentine's Day!)
Los Angeles, California

ACKNOWLEDGMENTS

I'd like to acknowledge all the people who contributed to making this book possible. I'm blessed to have so many people in my personal and professional life who share my vision and help turn my ideas into realities.

Kevin "SK" Simon, my husband.

Gloria R Green, my mother.

DeOnzell Green, my sister.

Nidhi Lucky Handa, my manager.

Leslie Miranda, my best friend.

Google/YouTube, my platform.

GloBugZ, my fans.

Byrd Leavell, my literary agent.

Nils Parker, my coauthor.

Christine Aprile, my assistant.

Luke Dempsey and the HarperOne team, my publisher.